Freedom and Shackles

Viktor

Viktor – Spiritual Teachings

Copyright © 2024 Ragnar Viktor Karlsson

All rights reserved.

ISBN 979-8883-21-334-1

Table of Contents

Chapter 1 Earth and Environment	1
Chapter 2 Man and His Evolution	9
Chapter 3 Beginnings of Community	17
Chapter 4 Human Nature	25
Chapter 5 Visible Power	33
Chapter 6 Diminishing Freedom	39
Chapter 7 Freedom and the Soul	47
Chapter 8 Power over the Mind	55
Chapter 9 Money and Power	63
Chapter 10 Concentration of Power	73
Chapter 11 Power and the Age of Souls	81
Chapter 12 The Way to Freedom	87
Chapter 13 The Inner Power	97
Chapter 14 Spiritual Awakening	107
Chapter 15 The Truth	119
Chapter 16 Love	125
Chapter 17 Unity	129
Chapter 18 Time of Changing	137
Chapter 19 Transformations	145
Chapter 20 The True Spiritual Teacher	155

| Chapter 21 New Eras | 163 |
| Chapter 22 The Unity of All That Is | 171 |

Chapter 1

Earth and Environment

Earth, man, animals, and nature are God's creation, and all are one. Man is part of the earth and everything that exists. The earth was created so that man's soul can develop and experience all that earthly life has to offer. Wildlife and nature give man diversity and different experiences during his development. Man is born free and has free will, and all paths are open to him. The earth and all that it yields can be said to be God's gifts meant for man so that he can live and prosper here on earth. The earth provides mankind with water, nutrition, energy, and everything he needs during his stay on earth. Each person's stay here is temporary, with a beginning and an end. In order for man to experience all that earthly life has to offer, the soul is incarnated hundreds of times, and the experience differs from life to life. No one owns anything on earth—everything is borrowed during their stay.

The earth is created so that everything is a cycle and there is enough for everyone everywhere. The simplicity of wildlife and nature, where everything runs in a natural cycle without external interference, is a manifestation of creation

Viktor

in its simplest form. The animals and vegetation adapt to different conditions and seasons. Each one stays in the places on earth that suit it, be they animals, flora, or humans. The animals choose places to stay where the environment and climate are suitable. The same applies to vegetation: each plant grows and thrives in the climate that suits it. The climate and environment vary here on earth, and each chooses his or her own region in which to stay. Weather and its variations are created to give this diversity to our environment. Some areas are cold with severe weather variations, while others are hot and have very balanced weather all year round. There are no coincidences in creation, and everything is created so that it is possible to gain maximum diversity in one's surroundings and existence. It is the age of the soul that determines what kind of environment a person wants to live in at any given time, and this changes from life to life. The needs of the souls are different, and it differs from what the soul wants to experience at any given time. The earth and creation are created in such a way to satisfy all the needs of the soul in its development process, spanning many lives and many centuries. Man's connection to nature varies according to the age of the soul. The youngest and oldest souls aspire to nature, while the young souls are more preoccupied with fame and fortune, so they often choose to stay in cities among crowds. But nothing is universal, and the needs are different for each one.

It is not only the diversity of the earth and nature that creates diversity for the soul, but also the national psyche

Freedom and Shackles

of each country. Each nation has its own culture, history, legal system, and form of government that differ from other nations. Before the soul incarnates here on earth, it chooses a country of birth that suits its maturity path and the tasks it intends to solve and go through in the life to come. Climate and nature are the deciding factor in that choice, but it is influenced by the nation and the national psyche. Therefore, diversity among countries is essential for the soul to experience different conditions in each life. In this way, the soul develops and experiences all that earthly life has to offer. History, culture, and language connect the people and shape and create the national psyche in each country. Some countries are peaceful and have few inhabitants, such that the soul gets to experience freedom and vastness and a life without conflict or war, while other countries are crowded with a lot of people and the density is high. It is a challenge for the soul to be around crowds for long periods of time, testing and training tolerance and intimacy with other people. There are countries with high rates of crime, theft, and other forms of violence. There are also countries that are war-torn, where the soul experiences destruction and even hunger and destitution. All these different environments are suited and designed for the soul to experience great diversity. Therefore, the location and country of birth of the soul are carefully chosen before the soul reaches earth.

The national psyche of each country is slowly changing and evolving as the average age of souls increases. The baby souls often live in war-torn countries with a lot of

Viktor

natural disasters taking place, while the old souls prefer to live in peaceful and relatively small countries. Nothing is universal, and old souls as well as children's souls are scattered all over the earth. Some souls choose to move between countries in their middle age, thus experiencing different cultures in the same life. It is important that each nation is allowed to develop at its own pace and in its own way. Such developments need to take place normally, without external disturbances, yet they can be broken down in a short period of time if one nation invades another and begins to transform its regime and culture. Such transformation is a forced action that not only destroys nature and people's worldly possessions but also degrades and destroys centuries-old civilization. Many ignore and forget this part of the devastation that occurs in wars when one nation invades another. It is most successful when everything here on earth, whether it be the earth itself, nature, the animal kingdom, the national souls, or the soul itself, is allowed to evolve, grow, and prosper in its natural way without external disturbances.

The solar system and everything in it have a profound impact on earth and all life on earth. Without the sun, there would be little life on earth but eternal darkness and cold. The sun is a great source of energy that gives life, light, and warmth to the earth and all that is on it. The distance between the earth and the sun is designed in such a way that the right temperature is generated for man, the animal kingdom, plants, and vegetation. Everything is designed in such a way that the different varieties of flora and the

Freedom and Shackles

animal kingdom can thrive on earth. The distance between the earth and the sun varies with the time of year, creating the seasons, which produces diversity and necessary cycles for flora, animals, and humans. All earthly life follows a cycle, whether it be the seasons or the daily life of each of everyone. In the northern hemisphere, flora and parts of the fauna hibernate during the winter, and then wake up again in spring and bloom and enjoy themselves in summer in sun and heat.

The planets in the solar system have a profound influence on the energy here on earth, and this energy creates distinct periods for mankind. The planetary cycle spans thousands of years, making each period in human history several centuries long. This energy affects the well-being of man here on earth as well as the earth itself. The energy that has prevailed on earth over the last centuries has led to deception and betrayal between people. For the most part, man has been blind to the truth in his surroundings and to himself. This has led to a lot of fear within many. When this period unfolds, truth will come to the surface and transformations will take place for man and the earth and all that lives on it. Reading the stars and the sky is an entire discipline, and people have spent centuries reading into the sky and recognizing the vast context of the star system. Everything in the universe has a purpose, everything is connected to each other and supports each other and creates the necessary whole for life to exist naturally, and everything is part of creation and follows its laws. The solar system and everything in it follow a cycle that allows us to survive and thrive in the environment we are in. Everything is tailored to each person's needs, be it the earth itself, man, the animal kingdom, vegetation, energy, or water. All the earth's resources, including water, energy, and food, are inexhaustible; they are not destroyed but rather follow an eternal cycle. It is the sun, stars, and planets in the solar system that create this cycle of seasons, light, and darkness, producing that diversity here on earth so that everyone and everything can thrive in the best possible way.

The earth is a living creature that needs to be nurtured. It is sustainable and produces these products so that all life on it can thrive, whether in the form of water, solid food, or energy. All that is on earth comes from the basic materials of the earth, be they things and structures or the bodies of animals and men. All of this is what the earth yields. It is man's work to nurture the earth so that it can thrive and flourish. The farmer who neglects his fields receives little or no harvest, while he who tends the earth will reap what he has sown to the ground. When the farmer cultivates his land, he is nourishing the earth and its cycle, thus keeping the ground in balance. It is therefore important for man to respect and nurture the earth. It is she who brings us life and all the things we need to thrive in our bodies.

We need to be respected and treated well with the resources that the earth brings, and no one should absorb more than they need. When man mistreats the earth and its

Freedom and Shackles

resources, the earth and nature react, and natural disasters can occur as well as severe storms. This is a sign that the earth is complaining about human aggression. Crop failure is also an example of this. All of these are examples of the earth's cycle being destabilized in certain places, leading the earth to react in any way it can. Man tends to misuse resources when greed arises and to absorb more than is needed. This also applies when wars and explosions occur in certain areas of the planet. War in a distant land can trigger natural disasters on the other side of the world in the form of earthquakes and volcanic eruptions. Abuse and abandonment of the earth and its resources always manifests itself in one way or another, regardless of where it happens. It is man's task to make the best use of them and to divide them in a brotherly manner among themselves. No one has to suffer from deprivation whatsoever here on earth. It is the task of every generation to walk the earth and its resources with respect so that the earth and its cycles are always in balance. It is important that the farmers cultivate the land so that the normal balance is maintained. Man must therefore be aware that the earth is a living being that needs to be treated well and with respect. What are the needs of the earth? What is it that humans do to make the earth complain and strike back? Man must have the maturity to live in harmony with himself, the animal kingdom, the flora, and the earth itself. To live in peace, to cultivate the land, and to exploit the earth's resources without greed and aggression is the path to balance for the earth and all that is on it

Chapter 2

Man and His Evolution

The human being is a spiritual being; he is a soul that comes from the energy of God, which is the unity of all things. The core of the soul is truth, love, and unity, and it is a part of everything that is. The soul incarnates here on earth to experience its opposites, which are deception, fear, and division. It incarnates hundreds of times on earth until it returns to God's energy with all the experiences from its different lives here on earth. It is the task of each soul to eventually find the way to God's energy and thereby complete its earthly life. When man dies, the body goes back to earth where it came from, while the soul goes to the Astral Realm where it stays between lives. This is also part of the development process of the soul in which it learns from the life it was completing. Then the next life is planned, and the soul is reincarnated on earth and now takes on new and different tasks than it did in the previous life. This cycle continues until the individual awakens to self-consciousness and begins to search for his way home to God's energy.

Individuals' attitudes change with the aging of souls. On the face of it, God's energy and true self are hidden and

Viktor

the individual lives in great deception and fear, and self-deception is great for many. Gradually, the person's truth and love grow, and they get closer and closer to their true self. Tolerance and charity increase with the age of souls, as does the importance of communication with others. The secular receives less and less importance as the soul matures. It is spiritual development that raises man's consciousness, which brings him closer and closer to the energy of God. Everyone needs to see through the illusions of the world and, not least, to see through self-deception, which is an essential part of human life. Man creates great fear and distress for himself, fears that do not really exist anywhere else but in each person's mind. Seeing through the illusions and overcoming fear is the task of each and every person. In this way, man gains true freedom—freedom from himself and others.

When the first group of souls came out of God's energy and began to form themselves on earth, man was primitive and different from what he is today. Souls that have newly come from God's energy and are living their first lives here on earth are disoriented and uncertain. They have a strong connection to nature and prefer to live in mild and even climates. They live in groups and take advantage of all that the earth has to offer. Emotional attachment to others is limited, and their attitude is one of survival. They are plentiful and do not absorb more than is needed at any given time. They live in groups that choose to live alone and remotely from others. This first period is called the Stone Age period, in which man began to learn

Freedom and Shackles

to take advantage of what the earth has to offer, and gradually to equip himself with tools to ease his tasks. He learned to find shelter, and gradually to cultivate the land and animals and start farming. With the age of souls rising, human attitudes change and technology increases. Knowledge and know-how pass from one generation to the next, and as technology gradually develops, human work becomes lighter and productivity increases. As the soul ages, there is a stronger emotional connection with others, and one becomes more interested in communicating with others. This is how society gradually evolves and cities are created.

As the soul matures, it finally moves from an infant soul to a baby soul, needing discipline and regulation so it feels comfortable and safe. This can be compared to a small child who is learning to shape himself in life and receives the discipline and care of his parents. As humans begin to live in larger groups and societies take shape, there comes the need to set up laws and regulations to uphold the discipline of the baby souls who actually call for such things so that they can thrive comfortably. From this need, authorities and dominant powers begin to evolve, with a small number of people creating laws and regulations to follow. Soon, people are being convicted of disobeying the law, leading to the people and the masses becoming more and more law-abiding. Children's souls love regulation and wish to keep things in order.

Viktor

Gradually, society develops and grows steadily. In the beginning, human needs are small: water, food, clothing, and shelter. Man makes better and better use of what the earth has to offer, fruits and vegetables and meat. As the first souls mature into adolescence, humans are given great drive and progress takes a great leap. The implementation and drive increase, and cities and communities grow rapidly. Technology advances, and humans equip more tools and tools to ease their jobs. The attitude of young souls is that life is a competition with the goal of getting and owning more than one's neighbor. Greed increases and people begin to absorb more than is needed. This leads people to start defending their possessions, as many have begun reaching for other people's possessions to gain more things and more power over others. Each community gets strong members of the group to defend against aggression and predation from other communities, and thus the military is formed and war efforts begin. Humans have been fighting for territory and power for a very long time, to secure their possessions and territories, and to gain power and control over the property of others. The young soul can be ruthless in achieving its goals and in winning the competition of life. Kingdoms are formed around the armed forces, and in the beginning the kings are as military commanders, holding the possessions and territories controlled by the armies. This gradually forms an upper class whose sole purpose is to seize possessions from others. The power grab increases, and most kings try to expand the territory at their disposal, which is not done

Freedom and Shackles

without wars and conflict. The fear of losing power and territory is the driving force behind wars, and the war then persists among the people.

The young soul's attitude is that it lives only once, and nothing is after death but silence and darkness. Therefore, it is her ambition to get the most out of life. But the soul matures and finally reaches adulthood, which can be likened to an adult person. The attitude of the soul changes, and now communication with others begins to matter more than power, wealth, and competition. The family and family life begin to grow stronger and become the foundation of society. People start talking more, and intimacy and emotional connections become stronger. The spiritual part of man begins to wake up, and the person begins to awaken to self-consciousness. The soul begins to sense and feel that she is part of something bigger and more, and that is something that takes over after death. Life is only a short period of the long journey of the soul. Creativity takes over from competition, and great advances in technology and science will begin to take shape. Man begins to read the stars in the sky and to record the cycles taking place there. Mathematics and written language come into play, and schools and education begin to form. Man becomes a seeker and begins to make experiments and discoveries of nature and its laws. Man feels and senses that there are higher powers that prevail; belief in God begins to take shape, and from that, religion begins. Humans have always had differing views and visions of a higher power, thus creating different religions. As the soul develops from one age to another, new infant souls enter the earth, and the population grows steadily. The diversity of life here on earth increases with the increasing development of the soul and different attitudes at each age. Gradually, society and life on earth evolve in the direction known to modern man.

The last age of the soul here on earth is the old era, by which time the soul has begun to perceive itself well as part of a larger whole, and spirituality has become a big part of life and existence. The soul is beginning to realize that man is an eternal soul in a mortal body, and that staying here on earth is only a temporary task to grow and experience. The old soul has grown gentle and wishes to live a quiet life away from the worldly vortex. The old soul wants to enjoy itself in nature and seeks freedom from worldly amusement. The quality-of-life race is over, and wishes to acquire as many worldly things as possible are gone. Spiritual development and freedom are now more important factors. The old soul also has a great need to pass on its experiences to younger souls and often plays the role of teacher and mentor. It needs to share these experiences before completing earthly life. It has little interest in practicing religion yet has a strong belief in the afterlife and in the higher. It has begun to connect itself with God without any intermediaries, and it does so in silence.

At the end of the soul's life here on earth, the individual begins to awaken to self-consciousness, and a spiritual awakening begins, followed by a spiritual opening. The

Freedom and Shackles

individual begins to search inward for his or her true self and begins to free the soul from the illusions and fears that have dominated the front. Finally, the individual experiences God's love in his heart and attains enlightenment, and thus he has completed his earthly life, and the soul continues as a spiritual being until it finally joins with the God energy from which it originally came. All the experiences that the soul has gained on its journey through all its lives and ages become the experience of the whole. Every moment and every experience is an experience of the whole, for all are one and belong to God's creation. The quest of the soul here on earth as it passes through different ages can be compared to a human lifetime. In the beginning, the soul is an infant soul, helpless, and simplicity dominates. Then she becomes as a baby who needs care and discipline from older ones. Then she becomes a teenager who can conquer the world and is dependent on no one. Then she becomes an adult, and family life and communication are now the most important thing. Eventually the soul becomes old, which can be likened to an old person who has a lot of experience to communicate and has become calm and loving. This is the same process that each person experiences in their lifetime.

On earth at any given time, there are souls of all ages, which creates a great diversity in human life because attitudes and approaches to life are very different. While one spends all their energy and time on a quality-of-life race, another is plentiful, appreciates nature, and enjoys the moment to the fullest. These two people may have

Viktor

difficulty understanding each other, and many judge another person for not having the same attitudes as himself. One thing is certain, each soul gets to experience all that earthly life has to offer, and when it is over, the soul ends its incarnation and continues its spiritual journey. The soul is eternal and cannot be destroyed. No one has to fear life or death. The soul, human body, animals, vegetation, earth, and solar system are God's creations and belong to God's energy. The human body is the vehicle of the soul so that it can experience earthly life through the senses of the body. The earth, animals, and nature are the stage created so that the soul can develop and experience. The diversity is great, whether in humans or in nature, and it is the task of every soul to experience all the diversity that life has to offer.

Chapter 3

Beginnings of Community

Man in his present form has been here on earth for thousands of years, and many souls are centuries old, meaning they have experienced different periods here on earth under different conditions. At first, life was original and simple, with little technology and know-how to make people's jobs easier. Such periods were difficult physically, and people worked very hard to survive. There was a lot of collaboration, and people helped each other with difficult work. Most lived through subsistence farming and there was no money, but there was a barter system where people exchanged harvest. In this way, most people could live in plenty, and each had what they needed to live. The needs were not great—only shelter, food, and clothing. The fisherman gave the farmer fish and got meat and vegetables in exchange, and those who knew how to build houses for the farmers got produce in return. Education and teaching were simplified, with the older generation passing on their experiences and knowledge to the future generation. In this way, each generation refined what it had learned. Thus, technology gradually advanced and people developed tools and equipment to ease their jobs. Production therefore increased, and the construction time became shorter, and the quality steadily grew higher.

Most lived in groups, which is the first indicator that every individual had its own role in society. Some worked on clothing for the group while others worked on farms, cultivated the land, and provided food and necessities for the community, and the anglers caught fish. Soon man learned to bake bread from cultivated grains and meal, which was a major part of their diet. Most people lived in harmony in their community and contributed so that everyone had enough for themselves. The people were free and lived in harmony with others and nature; and everything was in balance, and each one had his own little land to cultivate. The needs and attitudes of souls are different, creating great diversity in societies. At this time, everyone had their own approach to things, and each person was drawn to the projects and roles in society that suited him or her.

Although each community lived in harmony and there was a great deal of solidarity among people, disagreements and differences could arise that led to conflict and violence. Then it was the older members of society, those with the most experience, who mediated and achieved reconciliation. Some felt that quality of life and products were misallocated, often leading to conflict and fighting. The older ones were able to calm things down and stabilize things, thereby becoming self-appointed judges who began

Freedom and Shackles

judging disputes that arose between people in society. Most respected the elders and obeyed their judgment in all respects. It is natural for man to have different views and attitudes that often lead to conflicts and fights, and this still persists. Most people in society liked living in freedom and peace from others, so most tried to maintain that condition, with each contributing to it. All differences and conflicts were seen as brotherly within each community. Although each community was self-sufficient for all the necessities people needed, societies soon began to barter with each other. There people exchanged food products of all kinds, clothing, and handicrafts, thus sharing ideas, inventions, and knowledge among themselves. In this way, the pace of advances in technology and know-how of all kinds increased. In order for the people in each community to live in harmony, the older ones established simple principles to follow to avoid conflicts. This was the first indicator of laws and regulations that have followed man ever since.

Although early life was primitive compared to modern ways of life and technology, basic human needs have not changed. In order for man to thrive on earth, he needs water, food and shelter, produced from the earth. The human mind is open to the indoctrination of the environment, and people can greatly influence the opinions and attitudes of others. The strongest is the indoctrination of the parents and next of kin, followed by indoctrination from those with whom each person interacts and then from society. Communication between people in the past was limited and was based on family, closest friends, and the early community. What could influence the mind was therefore limited, confined for the most part to the small community in which each person lived. Although other people and environments can greatly influence an individual's attitudes and beliefs, these characteristics are created first and foremost by the personality and soul age. The upbringing and environment in which each person grows up has a great influence on his or her attitudes and beliefs, but when the individual reaches adulthood, his or her own attitudes and beliefs take over.

The simplicity of early society created a comfortable environment for each one, and there was little worry. Each had their own role in the community and contributed to strengthening the foundations of the community, which was and is an enlarged picture of the family. Slowly, humans spread throughout the earth and colonized the different regions, and countries began to develop and take shape. Territories were later demarcated by borders, which were defended by the armies of the kings or emperors. Many wars have been fought by man because of borders he set up to defend his property and interests. Man has long feared losing what he thinks he owns, so he fights for his rights and possessions with blood, sweat, and tears. Fear has many manifestations, some of which often lead to the worst in man, and he begins to defend himself and make the wrong choices. Border wars and other conflicts stem from these fears. People traveled little in the past and were isolated for most of their lives. A handful of people traveled around exploring distant terrain, but most stayed in their own areas and cultivated the earth. Because of this isolation, languages began to evolve and take shape. Each region developed its own language, and later people had difficulty communicating with people from other geographical areas. Borders and languages are one of the things that divide people here on earth, so the soul gets to experience division instead of unity, which is part of the soul's development process.

After countries began to take shape, civilization and culture began to form in each country and the national psyche was created. The conditions, both climatic and natural, were and are different from country to country. Many countries are flat, and the ground is fertile and cultivation for cultivation are good, while others are mountainous with little or no land to cultivate, and grains, vegetables, and fruits can be difficult to grow. These varying conditions made the national psyche different, because it different circumstances and living conditions shaped the people. The national psyche in each country takes centuries to take shape and evolve. When the soul is born into a society, it grows up with and receives its indoctrination from the national psyche that prevails in the country in which it is born. It gets to experience and live under the conditions prevailing in the country of its birth. This gives the soul maturity, and it grows in every life, step by step. In the next life, it will be born in a completely different country to a completely different culture and national psyche, thus experiencing different things and

Viktor

environments from life to life. This diversity of national souls and the environment is therefore important for the development process of the soul.

It can therefore be said that life on earth has evolved in a way suitable for the development of the soul so that it receives and can experience the diversity of earthly life. After all, the earth and the environment are created for the soul to experience and develop. Over time, the earth evolves to the point where there are certain regions and countries that the young souls aspire to, while there are other lands where the old souls wish to live and be. The countries where the young soul is dominant have great drive and energy; therefore, these countries developed rapidly. The infant souls wish to inhabit a mild and even climate, so they aspire to live in areas adjacent to the equator. The old soul wishes to live in peace and quiet and enjoy itself without stimuli, and the soul tends to move further north as it ages, so there are a lot of older souls in these areas. But this is not universal, and there are souls of all ages in each country at any given time, even though one country or region is preferred by a certain age of souls.

This division also affects the national psyche and how each nation develops and is shaped. The national psyche is far more valuable to the people of the country than buildings and other structures. It takes centuries to build and shape the national psyche in each country, while constructing structures and buildings is measured in years. Therefore, the national psyche, culture, and history are the most precious things about every country, and it is the responsibility of each generation to preserve this treasure and pass it on to future generations. Although life on earth has changed over the centuries from original indigenous life to complex, technologically advanced societies, man and what is inside him have not changed. Indoctrination and what affects the human mind have changed over the centuries, but man and the movement of the soul are the same and do not change. Man's basic needs are the same, and the purpose of life is to develop the soul and experience earthly life with its advantages and vices.

Chapter 4

Human Nature

Man is an eternal soul in a mortal body, and there is nothing that can destroy the soul. The soul comes from the energy of God and is a part of everything that is, and the origin of the soul and God energy is truth, love, and unity. The soul is here on earth to develop itself and to experience its opposites: deception, fear, and division. In order to experience earthly life, the soul incarnates and perceives the world through the senses of the body. Human beings are therefore a mixture of physical being and spirituality. For a long time, the spiritual part of man is not active, and it is the physical and the earthly that dominate. In order for a person to experience himself as a distinct individual, man has an ego within, whose function is to keep the soul from its source—God's energy—and to focus on earthly life. The core of the ego is deception, fear, and division; it perpetuates self-delusion within each person, and many therefore live in great fear that divides them from other people. The ego is part of the human defense system, and without it, human beings could not thrive. Each person's personality or mind is composed for every life of the soul here on earth, which shapes and characterizes the person in every life. The personality therefore varies from life to life. Whether the character is determined or backward in his behavior lies in the personality. Greed, stubbornness, and low self-esteem also lie in the personality, and these are manifestations of fear. It is then the mind and thoughts that determine how people feel and live.

Each person's environment and life is an offspring of thoughts. He who has negative and evil thoughts nourishes the ego and neglects the soul. The ego then sends to mind thoughts that cause fear and anxiety in the person, which then intensify in the mind and continue to nourish the ego. This is a cycle that continues until the person wakes up to self-consciousness and starts channeling their thoughts into positivity and love. Then the soul begins to feed, and the ego contracts in the same way. If this is done long enough, the ego will eventually cease to control the person's life and the soul will take over, and life will be transformed. The person will begin to live in happiness, joy, and love in every moment of life and will be free from all fear and anxiety. The person will live in the moment and enjoy it to the fullest, whether at work or play. When this is achieved, the soul has completed its earthly life and experienced all that the soul intended to experience here on earth. This happens when the soul is ready. Then there will be a spiritual awakening and opening: the spiritual part of man will awaken from hibernation, and the person will live in balance mentally and physically. In the beginning and in most lives of the soul, it is the ego that controls that

Freedom and Shackles

person's life and does all it can to keep the soul away from God's energy, truth, and love. Truth is hidden and invisible to many—the true meaning of life, which is to attain spiritual maturity and higher consciousness. With rising consciousness, the soul gets closer to the God energy, which is the highest level of consciousness that each person aims for, consciously or unconsciously.

So, there are many things that determine and govern each person's behavior, and as the soul's attitude changes with age, the personality varies from life to life. The composition of the personality is often determined by the age of the soul and what it intends to develop and experience in the life to come. The young soul is open, bold, and unabashed, and often has greed that keeps it in the quality-of-life race. Greed is one manifestation of fear—a fear of lack—and is often a driving force in such a person's life. Enough will never be enough, and they always wish for more. Greed can be for money, food, emotions, and power. Love is far from the heart of the greedy person because that is where fear lies and acts as the driving force in that person's behavior and life. The old soul, on the other hand, chooses to live in peace and quiet and therefore chooses a personality imbued with an acceptance that creates a character who is calm and willing to help and teach others. Human diversity is great, and people are therefore very different in attitudes and behavior. This makes life an exciting task, and a big part of the development of the soul is to learn to associate with people who have different attitudes and beliefs. The very youngest souls often find it difficult to live in complex societies and can be led into crime and violence, becoming outsiders as a result. It is unlikely that an old soul will be led into crime of any kind. It is each person's task to learn tolerance toward other people, in particular those who are demanding and determined in their behavior, and to learn to remain calm and balanced in different situations. This composition of man and nature has existed from the beginning and has changed little or not at all over the centuries.

Deception is widespread, but the biggest illusion is the self-deception that each person creates for himself, which often leads to great fear. Fear divides people and can bring out the worst in them toward others. Fear is the opposite of love, so a fearful person cannot be loving at the same time. Therefore, a fearful person's behavior, words, and deeds can become malicious and hostile. Man's words and actions reflect inner feelings and conditions. He who is loving in conduct is governed by the soul and fearless, while he who is hostile in conduct is full of fear and distress and is governed by the ego within himself.

He who is in the negative part of the mind, with negative and evil thoughts, actions and words, and is controlled by the ego, will acts in an evil and wickedness way. This often leads to destruction of some kind and even death. Such a person lives in darkness and unhappiness, which is reflected in their behavior. It can be his goal in life to destroy and steal for others. The opposite is one who

Freedom and Shackles

lives in the positive parts of the mind, with positive and loving thoughts, actions, and words, and is governed by the soul; this positivity manifests itself in kindness and love that leads to creativity and construction. Such a person lives in light and happiness, and this is reflected in his behavior. These contrasts in people create diversity in human life and can be a difficult challenge to tackle. It is part of the development process of the soul to learn tolerance and remain calm and balanced in the difficult situations each person finds themselves in—to learn to act with love and kindness even though the people around them are malicious.

Everything here on earth has two sides or poles that are usually opposites, and this applies to human thoughts and feelings as well as natural phenomena: hot and cold, night and day, light and darkness, fear and love, deception and truth, division and unity. It is then up to each person to choose whether they want to be positive or negative, good or evil, tolerant or hateful. Everyone has free will, so they choose which side they want to be on in their lives.

It is in fact human nature that makes it difficult for people to live in harmony with each other, and disagreements, cruelty, and differences regularly arise between people. Most people desire in their hearts to be free and to live in peace and harmony with other people and nature, but this can be difficult in the long run. Wars and conflicts that have been here on earth for a long time arise from this negative part of man, where the destructive power is harnessed and humans walk around stealing, killing, and destroying. Man's behavior, words, thoughts, and actions affect those around him, whether for good or evil. In this way, an evil person can mobilize others to do atrocities, and likewise a positive and loving person can mobilize others for good works. Most of the time, it is a small group who draws others along into mayhem and demolition.

Since man came to earth, there has always been a struggle between good and evil. Human history can be divided into periods of good or evil, of construction or deconstruction. But as the average age of souls on earth increases, more love and kindness come in, and more peace is created. It is each person's task to master their thoughts, actions, and words and channel them into positivity and love, thus engaging the soul and pushing the ego aside. Thus, the heart is filled with love, which then spreads to others, man to man, because loving and positive behavior spreads and helps others to do the same.

Regardless of all the laws and regulations that man has established for himself and others, there are universal laws from which no one can escape, and which everyone must submit to and face in the end. Everything you do to others will be done unto you; he who is mean and evil to his neighbor will experience evil and wickedness toward him. He who harms others creates debt, and likewise he who does good deeds to others has incurred a credit and will later experience good deeds toward him.

Freedom and Shackles

The soul incarnates here on earth until man awakens to self-consciousness and begins to feel and sense that he is a spiritual being, an eternal soul in a mortal body. Then he begins to open his eyes to the truth and see through the deception and fear, and he begins to confront his false self and ego. The person realizes that fear is self-deception that leads to suffering and distress. He pushes fear out of his life and opens his heart to divine love. In this way, man attains eternal happiness and joy. He finds the eternal treasure in his heart that no one can take away from him, thus freeing himself from the suffering of earthly life.

It is up to each person to decide whether he raises the ego within himself or his soul. Man therefore has two sides to his behavior: many are loving and helpful toward others, while others are hostile and mean. The dark side of man can lead to cruelty and suffering in people, and this is at the root of all the wars and conflicts that have existed on earth over the centuries. This side leads to division and destruction, thereby breaking down what others have built and created. Here on earth, there has always been a conflict between good and evil, light and darkness, but there are also long and prosperous periods where peace, freedom, and prosperity reign. This has been described in the account of Adam and Eve living in paradise in freedom and well-being until the cunning snake came and the good time came to an abrupt end. It is easy for man to succumb to temptations all around him and walk the broad path to destruction, then drag others into that destruction with him. It is up to each person to turn from that path and walk

Viktor

the path of truth and love to gain eternal life in God's Kingdom. Each is his own savior, and one should avoid being dragged along the broad path of destruction.

Chapter 5

Visible Power

In the past, when kings ruled over their people, they practiced tax collection and punished those who would not obey the orders and rules. The kings and their families were self-appointed powers, and once they were placed in their palaces with their families, they had the power, which was inherited by the next descendant when the king eventually died. The people had nothing to say or choose but had to submit to the laws and regulations from the king. Taxes and levies were adjusted according to the king's needs. The king's army was to protect him and his family from the people and armies of other kings, because they always tried to seize a larger territory by force of arms. Many wars were fought to expand the kingdoms, and many were killed and badly wounded in those conflicts. The subjects were made to pay for the kingdom's war effort without having a say in it. Severe punishments of torture and death to scare people into obedience, and the punishments were carried out in the public square for all to see, creating the greatest possible fear in people. The king's soldiers rode through the countryside, collecting the king's taxes by force and aggression, and those who did not obey and pay were punished.

The governance structure in which few people control the many soon came into existence, and it still exists; although the texture has changed over time, the basic ideology remains the same. The working man pays, with his taxes and fees, for the pleasures in which the high class lives at any given time. The distribution of the earth's wealth has long been misallocated, but it is in fact the right of every human child to enjoy it, whether it be water, food, or energy. The high class soon formed and began to absorb more than is needed, leaving the common man to live in deprivation and poverty.

The kings and kingdoms ruled for centuries in which power was taken away from the people by force and violence. When the kings began to sense public dissatisfaction and turmoil with the ruling regime, they began to fear the people and feared for their own power and property. Therefore, efforts were made to change the regime so that there would be more harmony among the people. This evolved in such a way that the people got their representatives to the royal council, representatives who spoke for the interests of the people and worked to improve their living conditions; this was an indicator of democracy that still prevails. This system has evolved over the centuries. At first, a select few were allowed to choose their members of the board, and there was no fixed mechanism for selection. After this arrangement was put

Freedom and Shackles

in place, people began to live in the hope and belief that change was now expected and that their fortunes would soon prosper. The regime that had previously prevailed began to soften, and now the needs and wishes of the people began to be listened to at last. The voices of the people had reached the ears of the listening king, but it was he who ultimately still had the final say and decision-making ability. In the days of the monarchies—certain people in whom power lay and who were in charge—nothing was hidden, although not many people were satisfied with the governance. Protests and riots were suppressed by the king's soldiers; the public wanted little to do with fully armed soldiers, and thus the king always retained his power.

Unconsciously, selected representatives began to form specific beliefs and policies, and their respective focus areas differed. A certain group of representatives focused on supporting farmers and agriculture and worked to improve that economy, while another group wanted to strengthen civil society and boost business. These different policies gradually took shape, and finally the elected representatives decided to form parties and blocs around their policies. In this way, their voice would be strengthened when they presented their cases to the king and to the royal council. These were the first of the political parties. When a representative joined any faction, he often had to compromise on his views on some matters, although he agreed with the bloc on most issues.

Viktor

Although power at this time was fairly visible, many decisions were made behind closed doors. The main policy was for the king to retain his power, and it would be best if he could enlarge the territory he possessed along with the number of people under his power. These views and policies were always superior to the welfare of the people. The interests of the king and his empire always came first when laws and decisions were made. Many times, there were great differences between the factions and even within the blocs. Many thirsted for power and influence and often did anything to get their way, and power grabs were the driving force for many. Most of the delegates' time was spent organizing warfare to enlarge the king's powers, and then taxation and punishment against the people were central to the delegates' discussion. The ruling powers quickly learned that the best way to control people and have power is to create great fear and to divide people. If the rulers created differences between the people, their time and energy would go into the conflict, and the rulers would have peace to increase their power and control. This method has been used ever since.

The dominant forces began to lie over the people like a dark cloud and to become more and more overwhelming. The king's soldiers were able to come to the peasants unannounced to collect the king's taxes, and the money and property of the peasants and people were taken by force and violence if necessary. Thus power was visible, and this created great fear among the people, who dared not but obey the king's soldiers, when they ride around

Freedom and Shackles

with no mercy in their collection. Many tried to escape this terrible power, but it often ended in severe physical punishment and even death. The taxation was not constrained and was often determined by the needs of the king at any given time. Therefore, the people never knew what to expect when the king's soldiers went off to collect their taxes.

Despite the powerful power of the king and the ruling powers, society began to take shape and evolve. Soon, class divisions began to develop among the people. In order to better control the people and better understand what was happening among the general public, supervisory bodies were set up to register the people and keep track of their numbers, ages, and occupations. The inspectorate was set up to facilitate tax collection and to ensure that no one escaped it. It was also important for the authorities to ensure that there was no solidarity among the people that could lead to rebellion and revolution. They had to keep people down by all means and extract people's goods so that the king could live in style in his palace. These views of authority formed when a certain group of people began to withdraw from the masses to exercise influence and power over others, and these views are still the guiding principles of the authorities. Back then, the authorities' goals were clear to most people because they were visible to everyone. Many accepted this arrangement and enjoyed life in their work and play.

Viktor

It is in the nature of every man to live free here on earth, and therefore the authorities act against man's will by their commands and prohibitions. It is part of the development process of the soul to experience manipulative authorities and learn to tolerate them and enjoy life despite the tyranny and violence of the authorities at any given time.

Chapter 6

Diminishing Freedom

Both culture and civilization evolve and are shaped in each country as the age of souls increases, and such development is very slow and takes centuries. There are many things that affect human life and nature. The position of the celestial bodies greatly affects the energy on earth and humans, and hence the zeitgeist at any given time. The earth is alive, and its energy and frequency also affect man's earthly life. But the development of societies and the human environment depends largely on man and his free will. Gradually, society begins to take on the form known today. Education goes from the homes to the schools. Barter is replaced by currencies used to buy and sell goods. At first, these are coins minted from precious metals, and gradually things start to get a price tag and value, whether it's crops, groceries, livestock, or croplands.

The number of laws and regulations increases, and people begin to be sentenced to fines and imprisonment for their violations of the law. At first, the law is meant to ensure an honorable and good society where everyone can live together in harmony with their surroundings and other people. Farmers and fishermen sell their produce at markets where people regularly gather to buy and sell goods. Later, trade develops, which undertakes to sell the goods of farmers and fishermen for a fee and payment. This is an indicator of the first intermediaries who have begun to take their share of the pie, thereby raising the price of goods for consumers. Subsequently, a class division begins to develop in which some people acquire more wealth than others, and fraud in goods and products begins to take shape. Instead of everyone contributing to society by growing food, building houses, teaching, or healing people, groups of people begin to emerge who start earning money by buying and selling produce from others without contributing to the cultivation or making of the product.

When farmers and fishermen sold their products directly and without intermediaries, they gained more from their work, whereas they now had to spend their time selling and/or dividing their products. The intermediaries quickly realized that it was possible to profit from the work and goods of others; this profession grew rapidly, and the number of middlemen would only increase. Eventually, it became the person who cultivated or created the product who received the least, and the price for the consumer steadily increased. That's how merchants evolved and the business world came into being. After the settlement of the monarchies in each region and the introduction of currencies, class divisions began to develop among the people of the upper and lower classes; the high class was

Freedom and Shackles

driven by greed and began to steal and take from the lower classes. The high class stood next to the king and his council. Instead of people bartering with each other in an honest way, there was a high class that had begun to take a large share without contributing anything. This practice of taking for oneself would only to increase, because the greedy one can never get enough or achieve fullness, and gradually people began to live under the yoke of the high class as well as the king. The time of freedom had now ended, and now few were governing many with hardship and tyranny. Although its methods have changed over time, this form of government is still persistent, with few controlling many through legislative and hardship.

Soon, dissatisfaction arose over this arrangement: people felt that the quality of life was misallocated, and the monarchies and the high class were taking too much. The kings and the high class began to fear rebellion among the people, so it was decided to establish a state treasury in which the funds would be publicly owned, at least in name. The people still had nothing to do with the state fund and how it was spent. There was little change for the public or for individuals. A long time later, it was decided to establish a democracy where people could elect state representatives to manage the fund and decide on its allocations. In doing so, people felt that they had a say in how the fund was spent and how the state was run. For a long time, however, it was actually the kings and their rulers who governed, not the elected representatives of the state. The high class and the ruling powers deceived the public to keep people down and make them think they were free and had something to do with government.

Soon, government began to be about having power and being able to control the people of the country, and laws began to be introduced that made it a criminal offense to go against the state, which people required to obey in all respects. Therefore, nothing had changed for the people in obtaining a democracy instead of a monarchy where the king was all-powerful. The government endeavored to draw up laws and regulations to keep people down financially and restrict their freedom in every way. People were also held down financially, which is a way of keeping them in chains. The state soon began to tax farmers in an organized manner: they now had to pay taxes on their cropland and harvest, and those who did not submit to state taxation were severely punished. This was the same arrangement that the kings had employed before the introduction of the states. The treasury passed mostly or entirely to the kings. Instead of cultivating their land in freedom and dividing their produce into other goods without any intermediaries, farmers were now becoming poor tenants on their own land, because whoever pays tax on the land does not own the land but leases it from the state. The same was true of the fishermen, and other classes that had formerly engaged in direct barter now became slaves of the state. The state went further and further in its tax collection, and people were more and more crowded. The era of freedom in which people could pursue their work and exchange their products without

Freedom and Shackles

intermediaries had now ended. The era of hard tax collection and deprivation of liberty had now taken over and was only going to increase as time went on. This is also a period of deception in which the authorities and the high class deceive the public and convince them that they are free, and that tax collection and deprivation of liberty are necessary and are in the best interests of the people. This period has lasted for thousands of years and is still ongoing. This kind of social transformation takes about three generations because the third generation is born into the new system and does not know the one that prevailed before. The generation gap makes it so that there are few accounts of the times that used to be, and the dominant are those who document history.

When people were allowed to rule for themselves and to live in freedom without external stimuli, things and life developed in a natural way. Technological advances made jobs easier, which benefited the whole and each individual. Each one fulfilled his duties and contributed to improving society. Then there was cooperation instead of competition, and people had more time to cultivate themselves and family ties. Disputes were settled in brotherhood and harmony, without judgment and law. The people were happy and all stood together as one, and if trauma arose, they looked cooperative.

Some people are born to be leaders, and that's part of their personality. Such individuals have perspective, and they have the courage, self-esteem, and trust needed to

Viktor

become a leader. Therefore, there is always a part of humanity that has a strong inner need to dominate and control others. If such a man is ruled by evil thoughts, and at the same time is destitute of love and tolerance, that is a recipe for a ruthless tyrant. If such a man has greed in his personality, then it can be assumed that he will gain power and always seek more of it. When such people come to power, it has a profound negative impact on everyone around them—all those over whom they have power. They do not govern with love and do not care about the feelings or fate of the people. They look after their own interests and take care of their loved ones. It concerns them little or not at all that the people they control live in deprivation and suffering. Such individuals have appeared regularly with adverse consequences and have left death and destruction. This is human nature in its worst form.

He who is loving and tolerant has no need or desire to control others. He guides and helps others for good. Such an individual always thinks of the good of the whole if he finds himself in a managerial position. He makes the decisions that he thinks are best for the whole, for the prosperity of all, and he works with the people and thinks about their interests. So, being greedy and loving never go together, because they are opposites, like day and night. The greedy person is likely to gain a lot of power if he is greedy for it, so the charitable one has a hard time in that struggle. This is why humanity has been living under tyranny in some form for thousands of years. The dark side of man that is part of his nature leads to such control. This

Freedom and Shackles

often leads to loss of freedom, suffering, destruction, and death, and it is the driving force of all wars fought by man. What can one do? When the tyrant transforms his thoughts from evil to goodness and from negativity to positivity, love begins to awaken in his heart, thereby causing the fear that led him to greed to disappear. He becomes tolerant and begins to think about the good of others like his own. This results in development and welfare for the benefit of all. Evil should never be answered with evil, for this leads to further suffering and even death.

But such tyranny over the centuries has resulted in the steady loss of humanity's freedom and human rights. It can be said that the regime that has prevailed recently has the whole personality and greed of the tyrant, regardless of who sits in the chair at any given time. A system of government has emerged in the world that is power-hungry and reaches further and further for the freedom and possessions of the people. The fear of losing power is the driving force of evil deeds. This system of governance spans many countries, and so many nations have been governed in this way. Surveillance has grown in the same way, as there are few things an individual does without the authorities knowing about it. The processes of deprivation and increased surveillance happen in slow steps so few people notice, and they are often presented to the people as necessary actions to protect citizens and their interests from evil, from enemies that do not exist. Deception and fear are used to divide people because this is how people are easily controlled, and this method has been used by the dominant forces for centuries.

He who is blind to the truth cannot see through deception and is filled with fear, and thus leads himself into obedience. He who has opened his eyes to the truth can see through deception, and he who opens his heart to love is fearless, no longer ruled by others through deception and fear. Such a man has gained freedom within himself; although the authorities hold him down, he is free and fearless within. Each person needs to free himself and open his eyes to the truth and thus become free from all things. Once the masses have taken this path, the authorities will automatically lose power and control of the people, and transformations for good will take place. Deception and fear will become meaningless and useless instruments of government, and humanity will regain the freedoms it once had, so that everyone can live in freedom and happiness, free from the tyranny of the authorities that have ruled the earth for centuries. A person who changes himself has contributed to changing the world for the better. Love in the heart is transmitted to others and will spread among the people; thus, the fear will fade away and freedom will be achieved.

Chapter 7

Freedom and the Soul

The authoritarian and dominant forces of the past soon realized that the best way to control the masses was to divide people—to divide and conquer. They created disagreements among people in order to stir up strife and conflict, and while people shared them, the authorities had the time and opportunity to create new controversies when the first ones ended. This mechanism and this method have been used by the dominant forces at any given time and are still in use. Regularly over the years, the population has had enough of the management of the authorities and has grouped together, and there have been revolutions that have produced transformations for the good of the people. In addition, the authorities have relaxed their management and given the people more freedom, but most of the time this has been short-lived, as slowly the rule of the authorities returns to the same pattern and gradually evolves into tyranny.

Society at any given time is built upon everyone participating and contributing to the creation of the whole into a community. For this to happen, people must have a certain freedom and space to act. The authorities have tended to go further and further to curtail the freedom of the people through prohibitions and laws, and also to steadily tighten tax collection. Eventually, people give up and society succumbs and fails, and this has brought about great transformations in our societies from time to time. Everything here on earth seeks equilibrium and always achieves it in the end, and the same applies to the governance of authorities and the dominant forces at any given time. Therefore, it is always the view of the authorities to impose upon people as much as possible without creating an imbalance and society giving in and failing. But it is difficult for the greedy person to maintain such balance, and he therefore often goes too far in his management. The self-appointed high class has always survived through the harvest and labor of the masses, taking possessions of others thus managing to live in prosperity at the expense of others. The fear of giving up and losing their lifestyle has always been the driving force of the high class at any given time. Therefore, the aim has always been to keep the masses divided and busy with their work, and in this way, the high class has been able to retain its power for centuries. The high class has always adapted to the changes and progress taking place in society. It has taken advantage of the technological advances that have emerged over the years and used them to promote its own interests and power.

The soul comes to earth at different periods and therefore gets to experience different forms of

Freedom and Shackles

government. Each person's freedom lies within himself, and man can be free within himself even though he lives in bondage to authority. He who has opened his eyes to the truth is not deceived by others, and he who has opened his heart to love fears nothing, neither life nor death. No one like that can control, because he is free within himself regardless of what happens in his surroundings. He knows that the body and material possessions are temporary things belonging to the earth, but the soul is eternal and cannot be destroyed. He who understands and accepts these things fears nothing, neither the authorities nor other people. But it is a great challenge for the soul to be physically here on earth, because it experiences great opposition to its structure. Earthly life is egoistic, with deception, fear, and division dominating all around. The authorities at any given time play a major role in driving forward the egotistical environment that exists here. The soul is always free regardless of what happens in the human environment; the freedom and bondage that each person experiences in his or her life is subjective. He who finds himself in chains lives in deception, but he who is free lives in truth and love. It is each person's task to free himself from the subjective shackles and to experience and enjoy freedom. He who falls into worldly temptations nourishes the ego and thus creates subjective shackles for himself. Whether a person lives in freedom or bondage is up to each individual. Freedom is achieved through a change of mindset; one who is loving and positive in his thoughts will eventually gain eternal freedom within himself, a freedom that no one can take away from him.

The authorities have always been threatened by truth and love, because truth leads to the freedom of the people. This is why Jesus Christ was killed by the authorities and religious leaders of that time. Jesus had begun to reach the ears of the masses, and he opened the eyes of the people to the truth. He gave vision to the blind, and he helped and taught people to open their hearts to God's love. Therefore, the authorities had begun to fear for their power; they were afraid of losing control of the people, so they took Jesus out. Even today, the authorities fear the messengers of truth and love, so they try with all their might to keep them down and away from the debate. For thousands of years, there has been a struggle on earth between truth and deception, love and fear, and light and darkness. This fight is still ongoing and has rarely been greater. He who is blind to the truth is not aware of this struggle and lets deception create great fear. The soul of the fearful person is not allowed to enjoy itself; it remains sideways while the ego is plentiful, and the individual experiences great spiritual suffering and is fearful and anxious, living his or her life in the shackles of the mind.

The struggle between light and darkness, fear and love, takes place within each one. Each person needs to conquer the fear and darkness within themselves and see through the illusions. What happens in the environment is a reflection of what is happening inside the person. Intense

Freedom and Shackles

internal conflict creates great unease, turmoil, and imbalance in daily life.

No one should consider themselves a victim of authority; rather, their actions and control should be seen as an experience for the soul in which it is given the opportunity to experience its opposition, thus allowing the soul to develop itself to a higher consciousness. The more fear a man experiences, the more love he will eventually reap. Each person must experience illusion to reap truth, experience fear to reap love, experience darkness to reap light.

Each man must always be his own master and control his own life and well-being. Neither the authorities nor anyone else should be allowed to control someone's well-being and life. Every man is God's creation of free will and is born with the freedom to act and travel. No one should give up freedom and let fear rule and guide them along the broad path of suffering and distress.

The term "selling one's soul" is widely used and has many meanings. One example of this is an individual who becomes a ruler filled with power grabs, whose aim will be to curtail the freedom of his fellow citizens through legislation and regulation. Fearful of losing his power, he constantly pressures his fellow citizens so that they remain in chains. The universal law "Everything you do to others will be done unto you" applies to all souls on earth, be they king, ruler, or tramp. He who does something will experience the same thing later or in future lives. He has therefore incurred debts that he must pay later. All debts must be settled before the soul can eventually return to God's energy. Therefore, whoever uses deception to create fear and division among the people is making commitments that take many lives to resolve. He has therefore sold his soul for his work and delayed his journey and return to God's energy.

Many rulers are young souls who see life as competition, and their attitude is that they only live once, so it's best to get the most out of life. They neither see nor realize that they live many times and have to pay for all their actions to their fellow citizens, and no one can escape it. They have fallen into the pit of temptation, creating suffering for temporary power and instant gain. Most souls go through the experience of harming others, and this is part of the development process of the soul. As the age of souls increases, you learn to be loving, tolerant, and helpful toward others, and all debts pay off. It is the attitude of the young soul that the mind and body are all there is, and belief in the higher and in God is often little or non-existent, let alone awareness of the universal laws that apply to all. This often leads to young souls being ruthless in their struggle for power, fame, and fortune. They believe that if no human judge judges them, they have gotten away with their deeds. Yet each person is responsible for his actions, thoughts, and words and must be accountable for them, whether in this life or in the next.

Freedom and Shackles

This is what the soul begins to perceive and understand as it gets older, and so people's attitudes change with the aging of the soul. An old soul would never go against its fellow citizens and would never interfere with their freedom in any way. This is a good example of spiritual maturity and a rising consciousness where truth, love, and unity become more and more dominant in the individual. The soul's debts are paid by guts and forgiveness—asking for forgiveness for their wrongs, forgiving those who have wronged others, and ultimately forgiving themselves and coming to terms with themselves and their past is the path to freedom. All souls will eventually go through a process of repentance and forgiveness, it's just a matter of time, and it is up to each and every one when that happens. This will happen when they have opened their eyes to the truth about themselves and others and have understood and accepted the big picture of life, which laws apply, and what needs to be done to return home to God's energy.

Chapter 8

Power over the Mind

It is the mind and mindset that determines whether a person feels free or in bondage. He who is open to truth and love and perceives himself as a part of everything is free in his heart, while one who lives in deception and fear feels divided from all things, feels shackled, and lives in suffering. It is the mind that determines whether the individual lives in freedom or shackles. It is therefore important for man to be aware of his thoughts and direct them toward freedom and love. The fearful one is easily controlled and strictly follows the instructions of the authorities and others. Authorities and dominant forces have been conscious of this for centuries and have taken advantage of these qualities of man and mind. Creating enough fear among people through deception divides people and makes them unlikely to rise up against the dominant forces.

To enact laws that restrict and curtail people's freedom and make people embrace such laws, a methodology is employed that has been used for centuries. The dominant forces create problems among the masses, and when the masses become fearful, baffled, and divided, the authorities come up with a solution that entails deprivation of freedom and further shackles, which the people welcome. Many are grateful for the kindness of the authorities to help them out of the problems they were in. He who is blind to the truth cannot see through this method and will be deceived again and again. He who has opened his eyes to the truth sees through the action and does not let it create fear or suffering. This is one of the reasons why authorities have consistently disliked the messengers of truth, who are eye-openers. The ruling powers fear nothing more than losing their power and control over the masses. The word "government" describes this well: "govern" means to have control over and "ment" means mind, so the word means to control the mind, or to have power over the mind.

It's up to each person to wake up and become aware of themselves and their surroundings. Eventually, each person will realize that the struggle is about the mind and mindset, and they will let nothing and no one control their mind or thoughts. The task is to focus one's mind on positivity and love, thereby gradually pushing the fear out of one's heart and filling it with love and God's energy. But these objects and perceptions are hidden from one who is blind to the truth and therefore lets authority and his surroundings foster constant fear. Many believe and trust that the authorities are acting in their interests and doing all they can to improve the lives of the masses. The truth is that the authorities have a task of keeping people in chains and in deception and fear because this is how the high class retains its power and quality of life. The fearful

Freedom and Shackles

person lives in great suffering and chains, so the authorities create great distress and unnecessary suffering for people. He who has opened his eyes to the truth sees the consequences of the authorities' actions and has a great desire to open the eyes of as many people as possible in order to end their suffering. But he who is not ready to wake up to himself and his surroundings will not open his eyes and will continue to live in fear and deception. Thus, the seer can often do little for one who is not ready. All the authorities' behaviors and methodologies have their explanations and reasons. The purpose of earthly life for the soul is to experience its opposites: the world of deception and the fears and divisions that exist here on earth. The dominant forces at any given time have ensured that such conditions are created for the souls here on earth. Therefore, nothing is evil and nothing is good; all is.

Everyone needs to be responsible for themselves and be aware of their thoughts and actions. They must avoid letting others control their mind and thoughts, be they authorities or other people. Many people have a great need to control and manipulate their neighbor and use various tricks to do so, so there are many dangers to avoid. So, it's up to each person to be aware of these things, to guard against them, and to control their own mind and therefore their well-being. Physical well-being and environment are reflections of the person's thoughts. Although the authorities use violence and tyranny in deprivation of liberty and in tax collection, one of the biggest parts of control is mastering people's minds and thoughts. This has

Viktor

been done by indoctrination through the school system, religion, and media after they came into existence.

It is common for man to seek illusion and fear instead of truth and love. The ego sees for a long time that the individual is more susceptible to the deception than to the truth. He who believes and trusts in the actions of the authorities lives in deception and has given up his free will and freedom—he has left control of his life to others. The mind and thoughts are more powerful than many people realize, so not everyone is able to be aware of them and control them completely without external interference. For centuries, there has been a struggle over the minds and thoughts of the people, which is reflected in the struggle between good and evil, truth and deception, fear and love. A person who controls his mind and thoughts has power over his life and his well-being. That man is free from everyone and everything around him, and no one and nothing disturbs his inner tranquility. He has experienced the divine within and has freed his soul from the control of the ego and negative thoughts. He who is positive and loving in his mind and thoughts cultivates his soul and accumulates his wealth in the eternal treasure, which no one can steal or take by force, whether it be the authorities or the cunning thief.

Love is the strongest force, and he that is loving in heart is unshakable because he is fearless and is not guided by fear. Love is threatened by the authorities because it makes the individual strong and difficult to control. It is

Freedom and Shackles

therefore important for each person to harness their capacity and strength by pushing fear out of their chest and filling it with love, and the way to do this is by being aware of their minds and thoughts and directing them into positivity and love.

If deception is said often enough, it becomes a truth in the mind of one who is blind to the truth. Repeating the illusion is an indoctrination that eventually takes hold of the mind and attitudes of the people, who then cease to have their own beliefs. The innate common sense with which everyone is born gradually fades away, and people eventually get fed their beliefs and attitudes. This is yet another example of how people give up their power to others and therefore no longer have control over their own lives and well-being. Deception has many manifestations, and it is insidious and comes up behind people all the time. He that has opened his eyes unto the truth hath a vision and is not deceived. He recognizes and perceives an illusion when it manifests itself, regardless of what manifestation it comes from. This vision and perception are here to stay and will not go away from that person. When Jesus gave vision to the blind man, he was opening his eyes to the truth about life and existence and, not least, to the inner truth about the meaning of life. Such vision and such truth give people eternal freedom and free them from the suffering and shackles that deception and fear create within people.

Viktor

The only true truth lies in the emotions, and what each person experiences is the truth for that person, as the truth lives in the heart. It is up to each person to learn to listen to their feelings and intuition, and to learn to trust what appears and is expressed therein. There are many who constantly try to mislead others and drag them down the path of deception and fear in order to control and profit, and the dominant forces are no exception. Temptation is also used as bait to drag people along the path of fear, which is at the same time a path of suffering and chains. It is therefore important for each person to be aware of their surroundings and other people, and not least aware of themselves and their own thoughts. Learn to listen to the inner compass that knows where you are headed and always points the right way. The mind can guide the person along the broad and easy road of deception and fear, a road of suffering and destruction, or along the path of truth and love, a road that is narrow and rough but leads to eternal life and freedom. He who is not conscious of his thoughts and is not in control of his mind will be tempted down the broad path of deception, while the conscious will not be tempted or deceived and will always walk along the path of truth.

There are many things in the environment that direct people down the road to destruction and suffering, and it is less common to find someone who guides people along the road to a life of happiness and joy. Therefore, each person needs to believe, trust, and learn to listen to his intuition and feelings in order to find the right path that

Freedom and Shackles

leads to freedom and eternal life. It is important to learn not to let one's surroundings and dominant forces manipulate one's mind and thoughts; each person has to take control of himself into his own hands. When Jesus Christ was in the wilderness and Satan came up to him and began to tempt him to follow him, Jesus knew that this was the broad road to destruction; he said that he did not want to follow that path but chose to walk the narrow and difficult road to eternal life. Each person must make such a decision many times a day in their lives, so it is important to learn to listen to your feelings and let them guide you. There are many temptations, most of which provide short-lived warmth and happiness because they are built on sand and therefore fall easily.

The battle for the mind has been going on for centuries; it is still ongoing and has rarely been greater than it is now. It's an uneven fight, because most people don't know it's happening and are therefore blameless and defenseless. The dominant forces are conscious and act in an organized manner to get the masses to live in fear and deception and thus to be easily controlled. However, many people do not realize what is happening and do not react. They live in deception and fear and feel shackled and suffering, without even realizing what is causing it. The harassment is intense and constant to tire people out and distract them, and this is another way to maintain power and control. These methods of control by the dominant forces go up because the masses are blind and knowledge is withheld from them. Therefore, the first step is for each

Viktor

person to become aware of his surroundings and to open his eyes to the truth about his surroundings, life, and purpose, and about himself. This is the way to defend yourself so that you will no longer be deceived and can push fear out of your chest and fill it with love. In this way, each person gains freedom, and the ruling powers no longer have any control over that person.

Once the masses have come to grips with this, the struggle will be over and the dominant powers will lose their power, and humanity will experience freedom again. Many who have opened their eyes to the truth, and who have a strong desire to help others experience the same, can experience great adversity and evil from others, as many fear the truth and may react badly when it appears. Thus, it takes courage and strength to be a messenger of truth in a world and environment based on deception and fear. But this is the path to freedom, to give vision to the blind and to help others see the truth in order to respond to the harassment and attacks that are happening all the time. In this way, the message of truth will spread from person to person, and victory will eventually be achieved without conflict and violence.

Chapter 9

Money and Power

While a man is compelled to pay taxes and fees and to submit to the laws established by others, he lives in the outer shackles imposed on him. For one who is born into such a world, this is a natural state of existence, because he knows nothing else. The authoritarian powers have, in certain periods, curtailed freedom and tightened tax collection in slow steps so that few people notice that their external freedoms are gradually being curtailed. Stories and events are also created that make most people embrace the curtailment of freedom and feel a great sense of security within themselves through tighter laws. It is natural for man to be free and to live his life without bondage and coercion; therefore, the present state of the world is the great opposition of what is natural to man.

Many people feel unwell and are overwhelmed by the current harassment that slowly increases. Monetary stimulus is severe, and those who fail to meet the obligations imposed on people by the dominant powers are severely punished. Money and survival insecurity provide many people with great distress and anxiety, and many live

Viktor

in constant fear for their safety and that of their families. Many people fear not being able to repay to the government or the banks, because they know that these authorities punish those who fail and aggressively pursue their collection efforts. This is comparable to when the kings' knights rode through the countryside taking the farmers' property and goods and calling it tax collection. This collection was made against the will of the people then, and it is still so today. Money is, in fact, one of the instruments of the dominant forces to control people's consumption and behavior. Keeping people in poverty through tax collection is one form of violence. The resources each person has at his disposal are determined by the dominant forces at any given time. Control is sometimes relaxed and sometimes tightened. Many people consider the purpose of tax collection to be to run society and provide citizens with the services they need, so many people pay taxes with pleasure.

At a time when people were bartering directly with each other and goods and services were exchanged without money, and with no outside intermediary, one was free and bondless. Then the money came in, and some saw a game of becoming intermediaries and profiting from the trade, thus avoiding contributing to creating and processing the goods and services used in the barter transaction. It can therefore be said that with the advent of money, the balance, peace, and freedom that existed among humans began to diminish. The intermediaries absorbed more and more, and their numbers steadily began to absorb more

Freedom and Shackles

than the person who created the value by producing the product. This caused prices of goods and services to rise continually, and more and more people could no longer afford them. This created poverty, and many began to live in deprivation, because there were thieves in the road who stole great valuables and disturbed the balance that had prevailed before. Later, the states were formed to manage the community and community services; then another intermediary was added, probably the largest one, as the state soon started collecting taxes that have not done anything but increase since they were imposed. This was on top of the intermediaries that had already arrived. Some products and services became more expensive than others. Humanity steadily distanced itself from the freedom and balance that had prevailed before.

To manage and control the flow of money, the banks came into existence, and they were the ones who produced the money that was later put into circulation. People deposited money, which was a loan to the bank, and the bank then lent the money to others. The bank profited from the interest rate, which was higher on borrowed money than on deposited money. The banks quickly became yet another intermediary in trade in goods and services. They soon began to impose sanctions on those who failed to pay, and their assets were taken by the bank. This was the beginning of the debt slavery that is still practiced, and the banks have steadily tightened their penalties. Instead of the carpenter building a house for the baker and getting bread as a reward, people now had to borrow from the bank to buy a house. The loan was for many years, and if people could not make their payments, the bank took the house, and the people lost their home. This gradually allowed the people to become debt slaves to those who controlled the money.

The changes that have taken place in society since people exercised the free movement of goods have largely been in the interest of the high class who have taken up the work and products of others without putting any hand to it. It has been this way for centuries, never more so than now. This debt arrangement creates great suffering, anxiety, and fear for many people, even fear for safety and survival. The monetary system that has been in place for a long time is a scam in which the bank and its owners will eventually acquire all the people's property, because the system creates new debt as soon as the bank puts new money into circulation. Every time the bank puts money into circulation, it is the principal of the loan plus interest. The only money that is in circulation is the principal because the interest does not exist. Therefore, more money has to be put into circulation to cover the interest rates, and thus the debt increases, and the banks and financial forces acquire more and more of the people's possessions.

Money has led to the few being given much power and controlling the many, and yet again, control is driven by fear. These middlemen, the banks, the state, and taxes have made the people bonded slaves in their own country. The freedoms that prevailed in the past have gradually

Freedom and Shackles

disappeared through prohibitions, and the people have become eager to stand up to banks and states. The trend has been that power is transferred to a few people, who then control the masses. As it was in the time of monarchy, government is in the interest of the high class at the expense of the masses. For centuries, people have passed on this arrangement, and most people know nothing else—they hardly know what it is to live in freedom and balance with other people and with nature and all that it produces. Freedom has gradually disappeared as the debt prison gradually tightens, such that few people notice that it is happening. But many people sense that something is not as it should be, though they do not know what it is. Many people don't realize that things can be done differently than how they are done today. The high class constrains people steadily in fear of losing their power. This is also a fear that prevails, but in a different manifestation from that of the masses, because the masses are afraid of not being able to deliver and of breaking the laws and rules that apply to them. They fear the sanctions that have been in place for a long time, though in different ways than in the past.

The trend in recent decades has been such that taxes and levies keep rising, while the services the government provides to the people are decreasing. The authorities regularly come out and persuade people that there is no money and that taxes therefore need to be raised to improve and maintain services. The superstructure and administration of the dominant forces increases steadily as

Viktor

well as the supervision of the people. The authorities know they've gone too far, and that this could create a revolution at any time. It must therefore be ensured that the dominant forces can defend themselves against such attacks by the people. As a result, all monitoring increases, and each person's every movement is monitored.

As long as the masses are blind to the truth, this system can continue, and the authorities' grip on the people steadily hardens. Most people who open their eyes to the truth of what the authorities really stand for tend to see themselves as slaves and prisoners and can experience great hopelessness and surrender. They can perceive themselves as victims of the dominant forces. It is difficult and shocking to understand and accept the world people live in and how the few have controlled the masses through deception, dictatorship, and predation. But he who opens his eyes to his surroundings has taken the first step toward spiritual awakening and eternal freedom. Following this, a spiritual opening begins, and the person begins to come to terms with his surroundings, with himself, and with the past. Gradually, the fear in the breast gives way to love, and the deep understanding of life and self gradually increases.

He who has been able to forgive the dominant forces for his deeds, and who has begun to have love for them as well as for all people, animals, and creation, is free for everything and everyone. He has attained eternal freedom, love, and happiness. He now lives in harmony with God's energy, and nothing can disturb his tranquility; he has

Freedom and Shackles

conquered the ego within himself and is now free from fear and chains. Authorities can be likened to the ego because they use deception to create fear and to divide people. The first step is to learn to accept the actions of the authorities, to forgive and not let them manipulate feelings, to become free within from the authorities and from all people. Then there is a battle with the ego within each one. A person who learns to control his thoughts and to become self-conscious will learn that positive and loving thoughts lessen the influence of the ego, and the soul will come back to life. Eventually, the soul will take control of each person's life as he or she lives freely in truth and love, in union with everything and everyone. Many have eyes, but see not; many have ears, but hear not; many understand, but receive not. All things have their time, and one thing is certain: everyone will eventually open their eyes and ears and gain eternal freedom.

Money and worldly possessions can bring out the worst in man, and many are willing to betray their family, relatives, and friends for instant gains that in reality provide only a short-lived warmth that will eventually cool off, leaving losses of friendships and family. Some go so far as to kill another person for money and property. Money is actually an imaginary value: it has no value other than people's belief in its value. The most successful thing is to keep everything balanced in your life and not absorb more than everyone needs, whether it be water, food, energy, or money and possessions. That will be enough for all the people on earth; there is plenty to exchange, because it is

Viktor

human division that leads to scarcity for some here on earth. All that the earth provides for humans and animals is circulating and never runs dry, be it water, food, or energy.

Many who have opened their eyes to the truth of their surroundings and the systems that dominate the world are still afraid, waiting for a savior to come down from heaven and help them out of the shackles and suffering they find themselves in. The truth is that each person is his own savior, so the way is to continue inward and begin to deal with the ego and darkness that lives within oneself. What people see and perceive in their surroundings is a reflection of their thoughts. The world and its systems are the creation of people's thoughts. Therefore, the way is to master one's thoughts and direct them to positivity and love, to come to terms with oneself and the past, and to learn to repent and forgive, thus walking the road to freedom and happiness. This is the way and always has been. An external savior may guide and lead the way to attaining eternal freedom, but each has to deal with the ego within himself, because no one else can do that.

It is important not to let money and material possessions create worry, anxiety, and fear; it is important to believe and trust, and to let each day satisfy its own suffering. Also, be careful not to let envy and deviance take hold of those who live in plenty. For he who is rich in material possessions may be poor in spirit and live in his own chains and sufferings, but he who has love in his heart

Freedom and Shackles

and lives in plenty has eternal treasure within himself. He who attains spiritual maturity and rising consciousness has attained great and true success in life. He has accumulated a spiritual treasure that no one can take from him. Such a treasure is eternal and stands on strong foundations; it does not fall when storms and shocks strike. This is the true purpose of life: for the soul to raise its consciousness toward greater love, truth, and unity. All earthly treasures and money are temporary treasures that flow into the sand as the soul leaves the body. Such a treasure is an experience for the soul, as the soul will experience all that earthly life has to offer before returning home to God's energy.

Chapter 10

Concentration of Power

It has been the dream and wish of many power-hungry kings and emperors over the centuries to rule the world, to gain power over the earth and all mankind. In the past, these men sought to achieve their goals through warfare and physical violence. Many wars have been fought to achieve this goal. This has created great ills and suffering for many, and many have died, whether in war itself or indirectly. Through violence and oppression, these men gained power and controlled the territories they crossed with great tyranny and violence. When one territory was reached, they moved on to the next, and so on.

What these attempts to dominate the world all have in common is that they have all slipped into the sand and fallen in the end. Greed always eventually falls; people have never been satisfied with what has been gained and have always wanted more, which always leads to collapse. Therefore, every empire eventually runs out of sand. All tyrants have had to give in eventually, and the system has broken down. Most of the time, this has happened from within because of internal conflicts and struggles, as unstoppable greed always leads to collapse. Everything here on earth seeks equilibrium, and eventually it will be achieved, although there is a lot of agitation and imbalance at certain times.

The kings and emperors lived in constant fear for their lives and were most afraid of their closest associates and subordinates, because there are always people who want to seize the power and possessions of others. Therefore, many kings fell to their own men who attempted to seize power. There have always been people willing to kill and betray their friends for temporary power and wealth. Such thinking manifests a lack of understanding of man's life and purpose, for this temperamental warmth incurs a debt of the soul that must later be paid back, whether in this life or in the life to come. No one escapes evil deeds in another garden; it must always be settled in the end. This is karma, a universal law from which no one can escape. The journey of the soul, from the moment it departs from the energy of God to its many lives here on earth and its eventual return to the energy of God, is in fact one coherent journey. Although it seems that the soul leads many independent lives, it is one whole and is in context. One thing leads to another, and everything a man does to another person, he will experience later on his own.

After many unsuccessful attempts to gain world domination through warfare and violence, the high class began to turn its backs on gaining power over the masses. For success to be achieved, it would be best for the high

Freedom and Shackles

class that had already formed to work together toward this goal. This would be the best way to retain their power and even increase it further. The royal families therefore began to bond with family ties, and the high class now stayed together and became more separated from the masses. The common man got nowhere near the high class and was kept at a distance. The high class built large palaces with pleasure gardens and had many servants to serve themselves and the court. At the same time, the common people lived in poverty and there were frequent shortages of food, sanitation, and shelter. A great class division had formed on earth, which was the synthesis of the high class. The public had little to do with the armed soldiers of the high class, and therefore dared not disobey the laws, commands, and prohibitions imposed on the common man.

This concentration of power made the high class stronger and more powerful than before. But no one wanted to lose what was theirs, and sometimes disputes arose between monarchies that were usually quickly disregarded. This is how times of peace were created on earth, but the people lived in shackles and poverty under the power of the high class. As before, taxes and levies on the public increased, and the freedom of the people was steadily curtailed. To avoid revolts and revolutions, the high class relaxed its grip on the public, lowered taxes, and gave up more freedom to the people. The high class felt that it was best to balance power so that the public would live happily despite unfair taxation and severe curtailments of freedom. The high class feared at any given time that the public would rebel against them and degrade them, so it was important for them to keep power in balance. Later, they decided to curtail freedom through legislation in very slow steps so that citizens did not realize the slow changes. Steadily, the freedom of the people began to diminish, and few were aware of it. The same was true of taxation, because the high class began to levy indirect taxes in the form of duties. The high class was constantly finding ways of exercising complete power over the masses and controlling the finances of the people through taxation. This was necessary so that the high class could live in peace, with a high quality of life and prosperity, at the expense of the poor man. The public was blameless and vulnerable to the plotting of the high class, which steadily increased its power.

A class division later began to develop among the general population, and some managed to become rich and wealthy. Some farmers acquired large tracts of land. Also, many became rich through trade in goods and services, and with the rise in educational attainment, a group of people formed who were well paid for their work after training in medicine and other scientific disciplines. This created well-paid professional jobs among the public. Thus, an upper class, middle class, and lower class were gradually formed among the general population. The high class kept a close eye on these developments, as it was important that no one have it too good or acquire enough worldly wealth to

Freedom and Shackles

threaten the high class, and this has been the vision and task of the authorities ever since.

After the high class has begun to coalesce around the common task of retaining its power and control over the masses, it has used various methods to do so. One such method is to keep knowledge and skills away from the masses, as these things could lead to the freedom of the people. There is much knowledge from lost civilizations that were further along the path of evolution than humanity is now, but nevertheless collapsed from within and went extinct, after which a new era ensued here on earth. There is a great deal of wisdom and knowledge about the spiritual aspect of man, how he can use his mental energy to gain freedom and open his eyes to the truth, and how he can open up and activate his spiritual part. One of the tasks of the high class is to keep humanity down spiritually so that it does not grow into its full strength and thus become uncontrollable. Former civilizations lived in freedom and without bonds, training and teaching people to strengthen the spiritual so that human beings could live in full strength, both physically and spiritually. But now, many people are spiritually closed and easily controlled by deception and fear. There are examples of structures on earth built by previous civilizations that cannot be rebuilt by modern technology, and no one knows today how they were constructed. The clearest example of this is the pyramids in Egypt and beyond.

Viktor

The management of the high class became easier and after a consensus was reached on its actions. Although there have been differences, the task has always been common: having power over the masses. The high class had become aware that to master the masses completely, it would have to control education, information and media, entertainment, technological progress, health, energy, food, water, religion, government, and eventually politics. For a long time, it has succeeded in gaining more and more power over these things that affect people's daily lives, and it can be said that all that is visible to people in their daily lives is controlled in one way or another by the dominant forces, which are hidden from many. Religions and political policies are good examples of ways to divide people with different views, as each group feels that their own opinions and policies are the right ones. Many wars and conflicts have been fought here on earth because of these divergent views.

After the upper classes and the ruling classes came together, their actions became more focused and they gained control and power over the masses in a short time. This concentrated power more and more, making their operations more efficient. The ruling powers began to develop methods to involve the people and cause them to accept the deprivations of liberty and shackles imposed on them. One way was to create chaos and then come up with a prepared solution that always resulted in diminishing freedom and survival. The high class and the ruling powers are always a step ahead of the masses, who are preoccupied

Freedom and Shackles

with their daily lives and tasks and are in fact blameless for the attacks to which they are constantly subjected. Whoever controls the flow of capital can easily create crises by limiting its flow through the banks and societies. This is done regularly, resulting in a large transfer of assets from the poor to the rich. It is important for the ruling powers to keep people down financially to ensure that no one from the masses gains power and influence. If everything were normal, then things should be balanced, whether it be the finances of the world or the lives of the people.

For many, it is difficult to face the truth because they find it threatening. Many people react badly when they hear the truth, refusing to believe what they hear and see. The secular world and life on earth is a world of the ego dominated by deception, fear, and division. The interaction between the dominant forces and the public can be likened to the interaction between mind and ego. The mind's negative thoughts nourish the ego, which in turn sends illusions and fears into the mind, which in turn feeds the ego. This cycle continues until the person starts to take control of their mind and stop the cycle, which creates a lot of distress and suffering for that person. Earthly life is a reflection of what is happening within people. The dominant forces are the ego that uses deception to create fear and division in the masses, which can be likened to the mind. This creates a negative reaction from the masses, which in turn feeds the dominant forces. The masses need to open their eyes to the truth and stop letting the dominant forces create fear and division through

Viktor

deception. This cycle will be broken, the high class will fall over, and peace and love will be created here on earth.

This will happen when people are ready to step up and gain the courage to face the truth. This proves difficult for many because the ego resorts to defense when truth and love appear, trying everything possible to get the individual to return to the path of deception and fear. The ego will lose control of the individual if he opens his eyes to the truth and his heart to love. He who is brave and steadfast will eventually conquer the ego within himself and experience the freedom that comes with it. Likewise, the masses will open their eyes to the truth, and then the dominant powers will react strongly and resist. When this happens, there will be great imbalance and unease here on earth, but with courage and determination, the masses will defeat the ruling powers and gain long-awaited freedom and peace. The struggle described here is currently taking place here on earth. Therefore, there is a great deal of imbalance and uneasiness taking place all over the planet.

Chapter 11

Power and the Age of Souls

The texture of power changes with the changing times and the prevailing zeitgeist. Centuries ago, ruling powers used physical violence, torture, and executions to exercise power over the masses. These sanctions were used in plain sight to create fear in others and make people obey, but nowadays they use mental violence to have power over people. This difference reflects the average age of the souls on earth. The youngest souls tend to use physical violence, which then decreases as the soul ages and matures. The average age of souls on earth at the present time is at the end of the young stage, moving into the adulthood stage. This transition between phases results in great imbalances and transformations. The era that is now coming to an end reflects the attitude of the young soul who sees life as a competition and a struggle to reach as far as possible on the worldly stage. Such a soul wishes to acquire as many worldly possessions as possible and gain fame and fortune. The ruling forces today are mostly young souls who have a lot of drive, and their governance is characterized by the attitudes of the young soul. The governance that has prevailed for some time reflects this attitude. As the soul matures and ages, it seeks a quiet life away from the hustle and bustle of the young soul, and therefore it is extremely rare for the old soul to seek positions of power. It can be challenging for an old soul to live under the control of the young soul who has a lot of drive and expects everyone to have the same drive as her. Therefore, humanity is under a lot of work at the moment and has been for some time. People work long hours to have shelter, food, and clothing. The old soul wants more free time and wants to enjoy life and nature.

With the aging of souls here on earth, the governance of the ruling forces will change. An aging soul means higher consciousness, and the soul thus comes closer to its origin, love, truth, and the unity of God's energy. This will create more tolerance, love, and cooperation among people. The veil will be stripped away from the illusions that have prevailed here for a long time; humanity will have more freedom, and each person will have more time for himself, his family, and his relatives. But before this balance can be reached, there will be great imbalance and uneasiness, as the ruling forces and the high class will fight for their power and quality of life. Therefore, there will be more conflict between the people and the ruling forces. Freedom will be further curtailed and people's financial viability will be severely reduced, and many will suffer while these changes are taking place. But these transformations are inevitable and have been in preparation for centuries without many realizing it.

Freedom and Shackles

Humanity evolves in the same rhythm as the average age of souls, allowing humanity to experience every age of the soul. Now the young stage is coming to an end and the adult stage is taking over. The adult stage can be compared to a person's spiritual awakening, when he begins to awaken to a consciousness of himself and his spiritual part. The spiritual part begins to wake up, and the person returns to his full strength physically as well as mentally. The individual then places more emphasis on interacting with others and cultivating relationships with family and friends. Material things and possessions matter less, and spiritual development becomes more important. The great transformation happens to each person who begins to awaken to self-consciousness and raise their consciousness to more love and tolerance, and love will reach them all over the world. Thus, the dominant powers will lose their hold and power over the masses, as the eyes of the masses will be opened to the truth and deception will therefore miss the mark and cease to create the fear it once did. In this way, truth will lead to freedom from fear. Each person learns to control their mind and thoughts and to stop letting anything outside do so for them. Each person needs to take their power into their own hands and stop giving it up to others. The dominant forces are currently in conflict and will remain so for a while to prevent this development of humanity. More deception will be used to exacerbate fear, and eventually the deceptions will become obvious and will not work anymore. The old values and old governance no longer apply, so they will pass away.

Viktor

The positions of celestial bodies and stars are the driving force behind these transformations. Their status affects the energy of the earth and humanity, and thus it affects the zeitgeist at any given time here on earth. Their cycle is counted over thousands of years, so the transformations that are now taking place happen every few thousand years. It can therefore be said that the times and transformations that humanity is experiencing at this time are very rare. These transformations and uplifts in energy have a profound impact on the planet, nature, and the entire animal kingdom. Everything in creation seeks equilibrium, and this equilibrium will be achieved after the current transformations.

The adult stage is also a phase of spiritual awakening when the masses begin to ask questions about themselves and to awaken to self-consciousness. Spiritual development is increased, resulting in rising consciousness. Instead of accumulating worldly possessions, man begins to use his time to develop spiritually and seek his origin. This spiritual awakening has already begun, and many people have begun to search for answers and for their origins. Execution and drive will diminish as the spiritual side of man is strengthened. This transformation will lead to dramatic changes in global systems such as the financial system, healthcare, education, media, and entertainment. Instead of people being deceived and having their possessions and time stolen, the truth will appear, and peace here on earth will replace the wars that have reigned for a long time. The authorities are doing everything they

Freedom and Shackles

can to keep the masses down and contained. Eventually, this resistance will come to an end, and the transformation will eventually go through for the benefit of everyone in all areas. Man will gain more freedom and lighter burdens, as well as more time and energy for himself, his family, spiritual development, and self-empowerment.

There are many souls here on earth currently who are here to experience and participate in these transformations, but there are also many souls who choose to leave earth because they are not ready to leave the current era. The journey of the soul is a slightly longer picture of man's life because the ages are the same in both cases, only different times.

The tasks of the soul vary from life to life and vary in demand and difficulty. Some people live a quiet and comfortable life, while others experience a lot of trauma and have to work hard for things. The soul takes all its experiences with it to the energy of God, where they ultimately become the experiences of the unity; therefore, each soul is important to the whole, and no one is greater or more important than another.

Chapter 12

The Way to Freedom

Although the high class and authorities appear to be great roadblocks to people's worldly success, and it seems that they keep the masses in chains, freedom is subjective, and it is up to each person to find inner freedom. All secular things are part of the earth and are a single spectacle designed for the soul to mature. Most of the shackles people find themselves in are subjective but can create great distress and suffering. The soul is eternal in a mortal body, and the soul is always free, for there is no one and nothing that has power over it. However, each person's mind can keep the soul sidelined for a while and allow the ego to flourish, thus activating the interaction between the ego and the mind. This interaction leads to a great deal of fear within individuals, and they perceive themselves as bonded and restrained. Fear can lead to great suffering and unhappiness. The happiness produced by the ego is transient, and fear takes hold again. The individual easily falls into temptations, which can put the person at a disadvantage and cause trouble. It is the mind and thoughts of each person that determine whether the person lives under the control of the ego or the soul;

therefore, the dominant forces aim to reach the mind and influence it, thus keeping the person in inner shackles and restraints. The dominant forces fear the spiritual awakening that is now taking place, threatening their control of the masses and thereby their power.

Therefore, the transformations currently taking place here on earth depend on each and every one. It is the task of each person to awaken to self-consciousness, to open their heart to the eternal love of God's energy, and to experience their true self in their heart. Whoever does this will later spread love to others through his presence, words, and thoughts. The only way to defeat evil is through love; there is no power stronger than that.

It is also important to have love for everyone, whether it be the neighbor or the dominant forces, as hatred and evil defile within and create distress and suffering. Revenge also makes matters worse, because in this way, evil continues to grow. Believe and trust that each person must ultimately stand up for his actions toward others and face what he has caused others through his actions. This is a universal law from which no one escapes, and it is designed to cause man to repent and change his behavior from evil to good. Hatred and revenge therefore do nothing but maintain the condition that has prevailed on earth for centuries. The task and challenge for each person is to learn to love their friends as well as enemies and to learn to ask God to bless them.

Freedom and Shackles

Spiritual awakening—opening up and starting to deal with yourself—is a big and challenging task; therefore, there are many people who delay it or even give up. It takes great strength and courage to walk the path to the end and experience God's love in one's heart and become free. But this is the struggle that each person ultimately has to go through, and it is his contribution to making the world a better place for all mankind.

What man sees and perceives in his surroundings is in fact a reflection of what is within him, and it is the product of his thoughts. This means that the state of the world is a reflection of the mentality of all mankind. It is therefore so important for the ruling powers to have power over the minds of the people to create the world and framework they wish for. As a result, the best defense for each person is to master and control their own mind and thoughts. While a person is controlled by the ego, their life is in a certain balance, even though they feel fearful and shackled. As soon as a person begins to transform their thoughts into positivity and love, begins to be aware of their mind and thoughts, and gradually learns to control their mind, the ego begins to resist and does everything it can to get them to turn around and come back in negativity and fear. This creates a great imbalance within the person, and they will experience a lot of fear and negativity because the ego inserts much more fear into the thoughts than before to stay in control.

Viktor

This struggle can last for varying lengths of time, depending on how quickly the person is able to master their mind and process the emotions that arise. Many people look away and give up, because this can be a very intense struggle. It takes great strength and courage to overcome this first obstacle to spiritual awakening and opening. With determination and courage, the person will gradually sense changes within himself, feeling how fear and worry slowly diminish and more love enters the body and chest. This perception gives the person the power and desire to keep going. Eventually, the ego will yield and the soul will take over, and the individual will experience a fearless life with love like a bliss in the heart. This is the only war to be fought here on earth—that is the war with the ego within oneself.

The frequency of the earth is rising, resulting in a rising consciousness of humanity; therefore, a great spiritual awakening and opening is taking place at this time, and many people are looking inward for truth, love, and freedom. This massive awakening has a major impact on the situation in the world in general. It can be said that the dominant forces and the media are acting as the ego and have therefore begun to resist this awakening that is taking place. They definitely don't want to lose control of people's lives. Therefore, they initiate a lot of deception to create more fear than before.

There is a lot of evil and imbalance in the world, and this is an enlarged picture of what happens within each

Freedom and Shackles

person during a spiritual awakening. It is therefore important that each person be strong and steadfast to resist the counterattacks of the ego, which here are the dominant forces and media. It is necessary not to be deceived by the media and descend into fear again, and to open one's eyes to the truth and thereby recognize the illusion when it appears. With the determination and courage of mankind, the ruling powers will lose control and step aside. In this way, humanity will gain long-awaited freedom and be freed from the shackles in which it has been held for centuries without even realizing it. People will sense this when it happens, and many will feel the difference between freedom and bondage. Like one who has been released from the control of the ego, they first perceive what it is like after the ego has stepped aside and given control over that person's life to the soul. The outside is only an enlarged image of what is within.

The way that each person awakens and frees the soul and activates the love that lives within, then carries it to others through his words, thoughts, and deeds, is the path to freedom, whether for the individual or for humanity. War, weapons, violence, and hatred have never led to freedom or peace. This method has been fully tested here on earth over the centuries. War and conflict only lead to more suffering and death.

He who has never thought about spirituality or himself and the inside, and who knows little about the interaction between the ego, mind, and soul, does not have the

Viktor

opportunity nor the capacity to deal with the ego through a change of mindset. He is trapped under the control of the ego and lives in fear; the happiness he attains is conditional and transient, and he lives in his own shackles. It is therefore important that each person open their eyes to the truth about themselves and all that is. Anyone who has realized this interaction is well on their way to freeing themselves. Then the struggle can begin, and the spiritual opening can take place. He who does not know this interaction does not set out in the struggle for freedom, because he does not know that he is living in chains. The same applies to one who is blind to the real aim of the authorities, which is to have power and control over people's lives and to keep them in chains: such a person fails to defend himself because he cannot see the shackles in which he lives.

The authorities in each country know how far they can go in power management and taxation before the people rise up, which differs from country to country along with the national psyche and the tolerances of the people. The authorities need to be aware of how far they can go without people rising up and starting a revolution, and it is the task of the authorities at any given time to find this line. When authorities go too far on people's freedom and finances, society eventually collapses because families, which are the foundations of society, fall apart. The dominant forces are aware of the spiritual awakening that is taking place in the world and therefore react strongly through the curtailment of freedom. The further the authorities go, the more

Freedom and Shackles

obvious the deception will be, and the more people will wake up to the fact that this is not normal. Then society will collapse, and the transformation will take place. Many souls are not ready for this transformation and will therefore leave the earth through an untimely death. In the same way, one who lacks the courage and strength to face the ego within himself will postpone his inner struggle. Most people will participate in the transformation consciously or unconsciously, and this is part of the development process of the soul. Each soul gets the opportunity to live here on earth at different times to experience the greatest diversity throughout their journey.

The road to life and to freedom is difficult, but he who has the strength and courage to walk this path will reap many things. Living free in love and happiness is really what everyone is looking for deep down, and many people try different ways to achieve that. Many people believe that worldly wealth and money are the path to freedom and happiness, but they are not. Such freedom and happiness is transient: it eventually slips into the sand and shackles, and fear eventually takes over. True and eternal freedom lies within each person, and spiritual awakening and opening is the path to eternal freedom. Learning to push fear out of one's life and to fill one's heart with the love of God's energy—that is the road to life and freedom.

The ego and the dominant forces are insidious, and fear has many manifestations and forms, all of which are convincing and manage to create fear within many. There is always something new to fear, and many people are fooled repeatedly. He who is blind to the truth is deceived again and again, and he lives in constant fear and shackles.

At first, the truth can be uncomfortable and just as frightening, and many people find it difficult to confront. Therefore, many people, whether unconsciously or consciously, avoid opening their eyes to the truth, because in that moment, everything in their lives changes. They start to see things in the right light and the deceptions become obvious, and this is difficult for many. This is really another hurdle to crossing into a spiritual opening. Each one will eventually be convinced that this is the only right way and will feel it in their hearts. At that time, the soul has begun to take control and to guide the person the right way, and the more the soul emerges, the easier the journey becomes. Also, beware of the false prophets who are part of the dominant forces and whose task is to receive those who are opening their eyes to the truth. The person who is awakening to consciousness may be uncertain and insecure and has not attained their full strength and certainty. The false prophet begins to teach and guide in the name of the truth to which the newly awakened person is open for, and then the false prophet slowly leads the person from the right path into trouble and a dead end. In this way, he often turns people toward fear again. It is important to learn to listen to your intuition and feelings as soon as possible on the journey, because this is where the truth lies, as well as the compass that guides each and every one of you on the right path to the end. Careful selection of teachers should

Freedom and Shackles

be made at the very beginning of the journey. Many will volunteer, but few are true. The deception is insidious and lurking far and wide.

Chapter 13

The Inner Power

The transformation that is taking place at the moment is that the average age of souls here on earth is moving from the young stage to the adult stage. These changes lead to great imbalances and upheavals in people's lives and especially in the governance of the ruling forces. The era of deception and betrayal is coming to an end, so they are doing everything they can to keep humanity down in the status quo. Therefore, there are a lot of deprivations of freedom and rising levies on the people. Recently, there have been epidemics, wars, energy crises, and financial crises, and it seems that one thing is taking over from another. This is done to create intentional imbalance and uncertainty among people. This has led to great fear among many who look up to the authorities and ask them for help and solutions to the current problem. The authorities come out innocent and tell the masses that the task is difficult to solve, but they are doing their best to solve the world's problems. But it was the dominant forces that started the problems without the knowledge of the people. This is done to evoke fear, and then curtailments of human rights and freedoms come as the solution to the problem.

The recent extreme weather events are due to the rising frequency of the earth, as the earth and humanity observe a rising consciousness. Once the changes have passed, everything will be in balance again for nature, the animal kingdom, and humanity. The ruling powers take advantage of these extreme weather variations and say they are man-made, using it as an excuse for rising levies and further deprivation of freedom. The dominant powers go further and further in their efforts to keep humanity down, but at the same time the deceptions become more obvious, and more souls wake up, and more people open their eyes to the truth and to what the authorities stand for. When a certain number of people have opened their eyes to this, then the ruling powers will succumb and surrender to their actions. It will then be possible to build new societies on the basis of love and tolerance. No one and nothing will be able to stop these transformations, for no power is superior to love. Fear does not thrive with love, nor illusion with truth. He who has a vision of the truth cannot be deceived, and a man of love cannot be frightened.

When the ruling powers have succumbed to power and ceased to control and manipulate people's lives, there will come a great time of peace here on earth. The war efforts of recent centuries have been driven by the competitive will of the young souls. Many people do what needs to be done to gain as many material possessions as possible and

Freedom and Shackles

to gain maximum power, and sometimes wars and conflicts are needed to achieve this goal. Taxes and monetary systems have been driven by the same attitudes.

The young soul also has a strong drive for development and execution, so much progress has taken place recently. Technology has advanced, and a lot of beautiful structures have been built. The young soul gets things done in its own tasks. Therefore, humanity has been under a heavy workload for a long time. This has led to today's family struggling and feeling a bit torn apart by these workloads and long working days. The young soul puts worldly possessions and fortunes first, followed by family and friendship. But now this attitude is coming to an end, and the time for family and togetherness is taking over. Monetary harassment of people and pressure during people's free time will be greatly reduced, thus giving people more freedom and free time in their lives. People will have more time to cultivate their family and connect with their relatives and friends. People will get to enjoy the technological advances that have taken place in recent years with shorter working hours and more free time. Until now, the high class has benefited from these advances. All the technological advances in all fields over the past fifty years have not resulted in a shortening of the working week but have yielded greater dividends for the high class. This will be corrected once the dominant powers have left, and people who carry love and tolerance in their hearts emerge to rule. The era of betrayal, deception, and fear is coming to an end, and the time of cooperation, honesty, tolerance, and love will begin. Humanity will gain a long-awaited freedom it has not experienced for centuries.

It is important to strengthen the families, because they are the foundations of society—if the families are not allowed to flourish and prosper, society will eventually collapse. The family life has suffered, and time spent with one's family is steadily diminishing. Parents work long hours, and children are away from home in school and daycare most of the day. When they get home, everyone is tired with little energy left to give. Many people are very driven and wish to work long hours, while others work to have shelter, food, and clothing, and to run their home and family. For them, there is no choice about whether they work short or long hours—there are necessities to run their home.

The monetary and banking system have evolved in such a way that people become more indebted every year, and the banks and authorities absorb more and more of people's wages. This means that most people are not able to shorten their work week in any way. This needs to change so that people and families have more free time together and the family can thrive again, as it did decades ago. Money is used as a tool to control people's lives through taxation and fees that have risen steadily over the past few years to keep people down and busy working. This is one way for authorities to counteract the spiritual awakening that is taking place here on earth. It is therefore important to establish a system that looks after the good of

Freedom and Shackles

the whole and not the chosen few as it does today. The systems of the world are built for the interests of the high class, and this is the guiding principle in all decision-making. This regime is hitting a lot of people, including their homes and families.

Most of those who now live on earth know nothing but heavy government taxation and bank lending conditions, and cannot imagine life any other way. The authorities, with the help of the media, are also good at persuading people that this is the only way and that relaxing this arrangement will lead to great imbalance and chaos, and the authorities offer a lot of explanations to mislead people in this regard. The people have been led to believe that this is the only way to maintain balance in society. Therefore, it can be difficult for them to imagine anything other than what has prevailed for decades or even centuries.

All changes cause internal tension in people—many people even fear changing their daily routines. Therefore, many are fearful when it comes to major transformations. But there is nothing to fear, and it is actually interesting to have the opportunity to observe the transformations that are taking place—transformations that will mean greater freedom for humanity. Love, helpfulness, and tolerance will increase steadily, and the spiritual development of the people will increase substantially, thereby increasing consciousness for most. When the monetary stimulus of the dominant forces finally relaxes, people will have more free time with their family and their loved ones. Quality of life will improve with greater cooperation of the people. External stimuli will also decrease, and most will gain more inner calm, peace, and balance. The spiritual and physical will become more balanced, and each person will gain more strength, mental as well as physical. Intuition will grow, and people will be better able to make the right decisions in their lives. He who has love in his heart fears nothing and makes his decisions in balance.

The indoctrination and influence of the authorities through the media has been great and long, which has greatly shaped people's views and attitudes. Many have been fed up with the information received, yet have not looked outside the media for information and news. They have thus given up power to the authorities and are relying on the media to inform and educate themselves. They have believed in the authorities and the media blindly and let them have a great influence on their well-being and spiritual development. Often the media plays on and stirs up negative emotions, thereby creating distress in people and distancing them from their true source, which is truth and love.

Deception has succeeded for a long time in keeping people in fear and distress; it has created a lot of harassment that is hitting many people, and many are about to give up without realizing why. It is therefore important for each person to assume his or her own power instead of leaving it to others and thereby letting others control their

Freedom and Shackles

well-being. Anyone who has the ability to turn off all the mainstream media for a few weeks will sense changes within themselves for the better. More balance and calm will be created, and their thoughts will become more positive and clear. Many people can't imagine life without the mainstream media and can hardly imagine skipping a single news cycle. But life goes on without this, because what is presented in the news is designed to keep people excited and afraid, not to inform them about what is really happening in the world, so there is nothing to lose. This is an easy way to improve your well-being and create calm and balance within yourself. When someone does this, the mind will be calm and intuition will increase, and the eyes will be opened to the truth all around, and later to the truth about the meaning of life and everything within each one. In this way, they gradually learn to take control of their mind and thoughts and to point them in positive directions. Thus, the heart and emotions will be opened to love, and he who does this will increase his spiritual development and greatly raise his consciousness. This is a true value and the eternal treasure.

The truth lies within each one, and therein also lies the wisdom of the soul. That's the source of all the true knowledge that each person needs in life, which will lead to a heightened consciousness. It is, in fact, the true goal of the soul in every life to increase its spiritual development and raise its consciousness, thus getting closer to the energy of God. It is human nature to have different opinions about things, so it can be difficult for each person to discern what is right and wrong when others are expressing their opinions and attitudes. It is therefore important for each person to learn to unlock the wisdom of the soul, because this is where the truth lies for each; in this way, they will not let others and their surroundings create their beliefs. Each person regains power over his thoughts and life and thus learns not to let others or his surroundings create fear and distress. Mental strength and balance will increase, and each person will gain full strength both mentally and physically, thus achieving a perfect balance.

As soon as attention turns to something outside the body, the mind begins to follow it, and the attention turns away from the inside. This can create an imbalance and lead to negative thoughts, thus gradually creating distress for the person. Therefore, it is important to find peace in the mind and look inward regularly to regain your balance and strength. This is how you learn to have power and control over your mind and thoughts regardless of what is happening on the outside. In this way, authorities and the media will stop controlling the people's feelings and stop creating harassment and fear as they have been consciously doing for a long time. Once the masses have done this, the authorities and the media will lose control over people's minds and lives. This is how change will happen and humanity will have long-awaited freedom.

Revolutions, wars, and conflicts will only do evil and will never produce the positive transformation sought.

Freedom and Shackles

Truth and love are the weapons that best combat illusion and fear, thereby creating balance, peace, and freedom for humanity here on earth. The high class and the ruling powers have prepared their defense against the transformations that are taking place here on earth today. They have used the authorities and the media to tighten power over the people through increased tariffs, curtailment of freedom through increased legislation, and creation of great chaos among the people. Many people do not realize these attacks and therefore do not know what is causing them suffering and distress day by day. The best way to defend yourself is to look inward and not let your surroundings affect your well-being, thereby harnessing the inner power that lives in each and every one.

Chapter 14

Spiritual Awakening

The soul comes from God's energy. Its source is truth, love, and unity, and it is a part of everything that is. The soul is the drop, and the energy of God is the sea; the sea is in the drop, and the drop is in the sea. The soul leaves God's energy to gain experience of earthly life, to be separated from the unity of all things, and to experience itself as a discrete individual. The soul goes from life to life here on earth, and as long as it is separated from the energy of God, it lives in sin. It experiences the soul's opposites, which are deception, fear, and division. One of the biggest parts of the soul's experience is emotions and dealing with them, whether they are positive or negative. It is also an important experience to interact with other people who are souls at different stages of development. Dealing with emotions and interacting with others can be challenging and shocking for the individual, but there is also a lot of joy and happiness inherent in these experiences.

The soul goes from life to life and experiences different things in each life, living in different places and tackling different tasks. The goal of every life is to attain spiritual maturity and slowly raise its consciousness, thus getting closer to its origin, the energy of God, in every life. These two are the only true and eternal treasures possessed by the soul, and no one can take them from the soul. This is unlike worldly possessions, which eventually disappear and flow into the sand when the soul leaves the body at the end of life. Up front, these things are hidden from people, but deep down, everyone is looking for happiness and love. At all levels, man is searching for his origin and purpose, even though this is hidden from him for a long time. Many believe that worldly goods and possessions create the happiness they are looking for, and others manipulate the lives of others as they seek power over them.

In the beginning, the individual experiences himself, his body, and his earthly life as all that is, and he cannot imagine anything other than this. When the soul is younger, it has little faith in the afterlife, believing that it will live only once and nothing will be recovered at the end of life. The origin of the soul should be hidden at first in order to give it the opportunity to experience all that earthly life has to offer, in all of its contrasts. Every experience and every moment of every soul is also an experience of the whole. When the soul eventually returns to God's energy, it takes with it the spiritual maturity and experience it has been through, which then becomes the experience of the unity of all that is.

While the soul is gaining earthly experience, the spiritual aspect of an individual is largely hidden and even

Freedom and Shackles

closed. During this time, the ego dominates and controls a person's life, which gives him the opportunity to experience himself as a discrete individual—without the ego, the soul could not be in a body here on earth. The ego is part of each person's defense system and is the origin of deception, fear, and division. As long as the ego controls life and movement, truth is hidden from the individual and love is conditional. The individual seeks happiness, joy, and love outside of himself, and therefore these things are dependent on others—they can easily disappear and lead to great distress and disappointment. This gives only temporary happiness and love.

The ego nourishes the mind and thoughts for a long time and leads the individual into worldly temptations in the material world. The ego also fosters fear and deception. Fear is the opposite of love, and the fearful person is therefore far from his origin, the energy of God. This creates negative thoughts that actually nourish the ego, resulting in more fear and more temptations. A person who lives such a life under the control of the ego often experiences great joy and happiness, but it is usually very transient, as is the love that depends on others and can therefore easily disappear with accompanying sorrow and distress. This pattern of life allows individuals to experience the full emotional scale, making life and its experiences often fluctuating and shocking. It is common to all people that they are in search of true happiness and love, but in the beginning they look for this outside their bodies. Many people believe that it is up to others to bring

Viktor

them happiness and love, but all of this is conditional and is only a temporary experience. Such happiness and love are not built on rocks but on sand, and therefore need little to turn into a failure.

There are many things in this world that are designed to distract the mind and attention from oneself, thereby diminishing each person's self-consciousness as he becomes distanced from his true self. Religion is one example: the person looks in awe at the person they believe in and puts their mind and energy on that person, and the attention is thus beyond the body and the person distances himself and the consciousness.

When a person begins to become aware of himself, his feelings, and his mind and begins to control his thoughts and therefore how he feels, this is called spiritual awakening and opening, or awakening to self-consciousness. Gradually, calm comes to the mind, and the illusions of the outward begin to appear and be revealed to the person. It can create great fear and distress when the person first realizes that the world they have lived in all their life is based on deception and they begin to see how just a few people can intentionally create distress and suffering for others. For many, this is a shock, and it fills them with fear about what is to come and what the authorities might find to do next. But later comes anger and hatred, and they can feel victimized and thereby fall into self-pity. This can be compared to a grieving process to some extent, where one stage recedes to another.

Freedom and Shackles

When people have opened their eyes to the truth in their surroundings, they have only taken the first step in a spiritual awakening. Many people get stuck in this stage and become preoccupied with what the authorities are doing at any given time. They have not attained freedom; their fear has only changed its manifestation. It is important for such a person to continue the spiritual opening and begin to look inward—begin to meditate, learn to empty the mind and take control of it, and direct one's thoughts to positivity and love, thereby awakening the soul from a long hibernation. With this, the ego begins to retreat, and its influence begins to steadily diminish. This is when the body's energy system begins to open and activate, and the person begins to be able to slowly absorb the love of God's energy into their body. This opening takes time, because the body needs to open up and adapt to this energy that has been hidden from it until now.

The most important thing at this stage is to master your mind and thoughts, direct them inward in a positive way, and learn not to let anything external influence them. In this way, you learn to be free from the thoughts and actions of others, and you will experience a lot of freedom when this happens. When someone does this, fear and anxiety subside, and more love enters the person's life. He gains great spiritual maturity, and consciousness rises with each step. His eyes finally begin to open to the inner truth, and he gains a deeper understanding of himself, other people, and everything. He begins to see the bigger picture and finally sees the true meaning of life, finally thirsting for more love each day. A person who experiences God's love in his heart for the first time breaks down in tears from the intense love he experiences, but these feelings have always been within that person, and now he has opened them up and activated them. This experience is the highest goal of every person on earth and everyone will go through it eventually; it is only a matter of time before it happens. It is up to each person when the soul is ready to return home to God's energy.

He who has opened his heart to God's love is completely fearless, and nothing will affect his well-being or disturb his tranquility. He has learned to listen to his intuition and is now guided by the soul, which knows where he is headed. The ego has stepped aside, and the soul has taken control of life. The divine has been activated within the person, who has now found the unconditional love that is dependent on no one. The person has also found true happiness that is independent and is built on a strong foundation. In true happiness and unconditional love, he has found what he has been seeking for a long time.

He who has been through his spiritual opening and is awakened to self-consciousness will no longer let any outsider disturb his calm or create fear, whether it be authorities or other people. He deals with the problems as they appear, so he does not worry about the future or mourn his past. He has learned to repent of his actions and to forgive himself and others, and he has asked others to

Freedom and Shackles

forgive him. The body's energy system and mind are now in harmony with God's energy and nature, creating a great sense of well-being within him.

The achiever begins to radiate happiness and love and to spread love to others through his thoughts, actions, and words. He has started to have a positive influence on the people around him and has become a herald of love on earth, whether consciously or not. In this way, love passes from person to person, and light will eventually conquer darkness. The deception and fear of the dominant forces therefore become blunt weapons that no longer work on the masses, who are awakened to self-consciousness and are full of love and happiness.

There is a great spiritual awakening and opening taking place here on earth at this time, with many going through this process. Many people are experiencing more love, and fear is constantly diminishing. It is this that alarms the dominant powers, who are currently trying everything they can to hinder this progress and development in humanity. It is therefore important for each person not to be deceived by the actions of the authorities or let them hinder their movement, but to persevere and seek inward love and freedom, which he who seeks will find. This is man's path to freedom and happiness: for each person to wake up to self-consciousness and walk his spiritual path, eventually reaping God's true happiness and love in his heart. This is the eternal treasure that no one can take from anyone. Thus the person is freed from the shackles of the mind and gains great freedom, strength, and stability. Life will feel comfortable moving forward in great balance.

This transition from living in fear and suffering to living in love and happiness is only a matter of level of consciousness; one has raised one's consciousness and lifted oneself from the fear and distress that can accompany earthly life. The highest level of consciousness is the energy of God, which is the truth of all things, the love of all things, and the unity of all things. He who has removed illusions, fears, and divisions from his mind will approach the energy of God, and the fearless will eventually reach all the way to connect and experience the God energy in his body. Hell and heaven are not distant places, but levels of consciousness that are all within each one. It is the mind that controls where each person experiences themselves. He who is full of fear lives in distress and shackles, while he who is full of love and happiness lives in heaven in his body. So, it's up to each person to decide which side they want to be on. This is how it has been from the beginning and how it will be as long as man lives here on earth. It's a universal law that no one can budge. The free will that man has, in fact, is the will to live in illusion or truth, fear or love, division or unity. Each person chooses where and how he disposes of his life, but eventually everyone will walk the spiritual path and find themselves and their origins. He who has understood and accepted that he is an eternal soul in a mortal body has come a long way on the spiritual path toward the energy of God.

Freedom and Shackles

The great love that each person will eventually experience in their heart and body has always been present and accessible, but it is up to each and every person when the search begins. It happens when the soul is ready and has learned what it came to earth to learn, but until then, the ego, deception, and fear dominate that person's life. But everything has its time of visitation; everything here on earth depends on time, including the soul's journey. It is important not to let the transformations that are currently taking place create fear and diminish or even hinder the spiritual awakening and opening that many people are going through. Many people are opening up spiritually without realizing it, and at first there is a great imbalance and fear as they awaken. The ego is trying to block the opening and to retain its control and its power, as the dominant powers are now doing to hinder humanity's great awakening. There is nothing to fear, for no one and nothing can destroy the soul, which is eternal and will always continue its journey, no matter what happens here on earth for the body, which is only a temporary vehicle of the soul.

Just as it is up to each person to wake up to self-consciousness and to determine how long the opening takes, it is up to humanity how long these transformations take and how difficult they become. But each person needs to think about and nurture his own spiritual opening, open his heart to love, and then begin to spread it to others through his presence, deeds, and words. This is what each person needs to do to change the world and contribute to

Viktor

this great transformation that is taking place. Hatred, anger, violence, and revenge will solve no problems and only make matters worse, and will in fact only be an inspiration to the dominant powers that will later tighten the shackles of humanity. There is no power that can conquer a number of people who have opened their eyes to the truth and their hearts to love.

Many people have come forward to persuade others that the systems under which the masses have lived for centuries are the only ways to prosperity for the masses, any changes will only lead to imbalance and suffering for everyone. Whoever says this is exposing himself—he is only thinking about the good of the high class he is serving, and he is doing everything he can to stop these positive changes. Many people are preoccupied with defending their interests instead of thinking about the good of the whole. But it has been so for centuries, and the period in which few enjoy the fruits of labor will eventually come to an end. The old systems have always protected themselves through deception and fear, keeping the masses down for centuries. Love, cooperation, and tolerance will find their way and become the dominant attitude here on earth when this is all over.

First, the truth will surface in every kind of deception and betrayal that humanity has lived with for a long time. It can be difficult and heartbreaking for many to face that truth when it appears, so many have tried to avoid that moment. This can be compared to a grieving process: it

Freedom and Shackles

will pass, and eventually everything will fall into balance and calm. Humanity will experience a new era with great freedom and well-being, something that the masses have not experienced for centuries.

Chapter 15

The Truth

Truth, love, and the unity of all things are the source of the soul and the energy of God. When someone understands and accepts these things, dedicates himself to living in truth and love, and feels himself a part of all that is, he will raise his consciousness, and eventually he will live in harmony with the God energy in his body. That man has found the Kingdom of God within and is free; he has found the eternal treasure of love and happiness. In order for this to happen, you need to wake up to yourself and to everything. The first thing that happens during spiritual awakening and opening is that the eyes begin to open to the illusions all around. The person who begins to wake up begins to ask himself questions about his purpose and why he is here on earth. He begins to realize that there is something more to life than he has realized up to now. He begins to question what he sees and perceives in his surroundings, and to understand that all worldly wealth and property are only temporary and actually borrowed in the short term. He begins to sense that he is more than body and mind. Many questions and doubts come to mind, and the person is thirsty to know

Viktor

more about himself and his purpose, as well as life and existence all around. Then begins the search for truth—"the truth will set you free," as it was said. To live in harmony with God's energy, one must live in truth and see through all the illusions in life. The greatest illusion in every man's life is the self-delusion that leads to fear, suffering, and bondage. To open the eyes to the truth is really the first step in a spiritual opening; after that, it is important to move forward and look inward, because that's where wisdom and freedom lie. The world situation that the person now sees with open eyes has been this way for a long time; the only difference is that they now see it through the eyes of the truth, which is obvious when it appears.

As the eyes open more to the truth, the deceptions surface one by one, and for many, this becomes more and more threatening. Therefore, many people try to avoid the truth and continue to live in illusions, because it takes great strength and courage to open one's eyes to the truth, and once they are open, they do not close again. There is no turning back: the person will now see the world and the world order with completely different eyes than before. He who knows the truth also knows the deceptions, and it suddenly becomes obvious when they appear. "How can you not see them?" many people ask after opening. The eyes first open when the soul is ready to take this step, and an opening cannot be forced in others. He who is not ready does not open his eyes, no matter how hard the seer tries to convince him of the strength and freedom in the truth.

Freedom and Shackles

It is therefore important to sow seeds for those who are blind to the truth, for they will eventually open their eyes and begin to see it in themselves and in life all around them.

Once the eyes are opened, the person often begins to look at human history in a new light and sees that not all things are being reported correctly. The person now begins to seek out mainstream media outlets, many of which are filled with deception to keep people shackled to the high class. There are many people at the moment who have their own online media to welcome those who are starting to open their eyes to the truth and to search for more truth. These media outlets vary, and many of them create great fear through doomsday predictions, most of which are mind-boggling, which are set off online and become amplified by each narrative. Many of these media outlets are organized opposition to prevent people from going further in their spiritual opening. So many people get stuck watching such doomsday predictions and get caught up in the fear this creates. There are as many opinions as there are people, and each looks at things through their own eyes and determines what they perceive and hear. Thus, it is important to avoid the false prophets who do nothing but delay the journey along the spiritual path.

The path leads inward after the eyes have been opened to the truth, because whoever has done so basically knows how the world and its systems work against people, therefore is no need to investigate it further. The next task is to find the truth about yourself and your purpose, and to

Viktor

find where you're going. The task is to raise your consciousness to the energy of God, and thereby free yourself from all fear and begin to perceive yourself as part of all that is, part of God's creation, the unity of all things.

The great truth for each person lies in the heart and in the emotions, and all that is experienced is the truth. This applies well to the spiritual opening that each person has to experience for himself in order for it to become truth. Until experience, it is faith that keeps the person engaged and motivates them on their journey; eventually they will experience, and then the experience becomes a truth. Faith, therefore, is important at first because it is the driving force that guides a person along the spiritual path. He who has seen through self-deception has attained great spiritual maturity and has awakened to self-consciousness, and such a person is free because deception no longer creates fear or the distress that results from fear.

Eternal freedom is subjective and lies within each one. The truth then awakens the love within, which wards off all fear. He has gained full spiritual strength and self-consciousness and can use his mind to control his life and movement. He has gained freedom from deception, fear, and division. A person who is spiritually ready and has attained the spiritual maturity needed to open his eyes to the truth will do so unconsciously. Gradually, your eyes will be opened to the illusions of earthly life and the systems you have created on your own. Everything has its time, and the hour of truth will appear to everyone sooner or later.

Freedom and Shackles

With rising consciousness of humanity, the deceptions of the dominant forces will cease to create the fear they once did, and it will no longer be a blunt weapon in the hands of those who believe they are in control of the masses. Rising consciousness leads to greater truths, and love among men will increase. Each person needs to find the truth within himself and learn to distinguish it from the illusions. This is one of the pillars of God's energy, and it is therefore very important to those who want to connect with the energy of God in their hearts and bodies.

Truth leads to happiness, love, and freedom.

Chapter 16

Love

He who has opened his eyes to the truth and continues his spiritual journey begins to open his heart to love. Many people get caught up in the first step: they spend their energy and time watching the deceptions of the authorities and the media and letting them control their feelings and minds. But this is only the first step on a long journey along the spiritual path. The path now leads to where love and wisdom lie.

Opening one's heart to the love of all things requires settling old feelings, sorrows, and anger that prevent love from flowing down into the heart. You have to settle the past and learn to forgive yourself and others. Dealing with yourself and your past is a challenging task that many people push off and postpone all the time. One thing is for sure, everyone will eventually wage this internal battle, and everyone will win in the end. This is the way to connect with God's energy and find the true home of the soul, which has been on a long journey here on earth and gone through many different lives on that journey. Awareness of yourself, your feelings, and your thoughts is an important factor at this stage. This leads to the soul stepping forward

Viktor

and taking over the ego and egoistic thoughts; as a result, the heart will gradually open up to more love, and at the same time, the fear will depart and disappear from that person's life. Living your life carefree, without fear or anxiety, is what most people desire and wish for, and they are seeking every way to achieve this.

Most often, it is emotions from the past, anger, hatred, and sorrows that prevent people from drawing the love of God's energy into their hearts, and it is also fear that overtakes the emotional realm. To cleanse your heart of the feelings of the past, you have to cry out old sorrows, scream out old anger, and then, last but not least, forgive others and yourself, thereby settling your past. To get rid of fear, the first step is to be aware that fear is self-deception that creates a lot of unnecessary suffering for individuals. Whoever has understood and accepted this is well on his way to releasing his fears. Then be aware of yourself, your mind, and your thoughts, and learn to calm your mind and channel your thoughts into positivity and love. Whoever believes in love and begins to seek will eventually feel and experience it in his heart, and thus all fear will be gone. The soul then begins to rise within the person, the divine begins to emerge, and the person begins to experience the divine within him, which is a great love and ecstasy of energy that will eventually flow through every cell of the body. He will experience heaven on earth, and this is what everyone is looking for, because this is the origin of the soul and the energy and love from which the soul comes in the beginning. The final task for every

Freedom and Shackles

person on earth is to find this love and this energy in their bodies. A person who begins to experience love in his heart fills his life with great joy and happiness and begins to radiate and spread love to others through his presence, his thoughts, and his words. This is how love passes from person to person, which will change the world for the better.

Truth and love go hand in hand, and truth wards off fear, thus opening up love in the heart. The great love of God's energy is open to all and has always been there, and anyone who opens their heart and feelings to it will experience it, unconditional love that will never disappear. The more love a person exudes for others, the more love they will experience. Love is actually a level of consciousness, like fear. The energy of God is the highest level of consciousness, the level that each person ends up reaching. A person who is full of fear and anxiety and is not self-aware has a low level of consciousness and experiences a lot of suffering and unhappiness in their life. Increasing one's spiritual development and raising the level of consciousness is up to each one, and this is life's only true and eternal success. He who nourishes the soul with loving and positive thoughts accumulates eternal wealth.

Chapter 17

Unity

The soul comes from God's energy, where it is truth, love and unity—all are one. The soul is part of everything that is. The soul moves from God's energy to experience and to develop and to experience its opposites. In order to live here on earth, the soul needs a body to be in, and thus it can perceive and experience what earthly life has to offer. The earth is an environment where deception, fear, and division have been dominant for a long time. Therefore, this is the environment suitable for the soul to develop itself and to have the opportunity to experience its contrasts. It is not possible for the soul to experience all that earthly life has to offer in one lifetime, and therefore it must be born many times here on earth. The soul lives many different lives under every imaginable condition until it eventually reconnects with God's energy and thus completes its earthly life. The ego dominates the person's life at first, but gradually the soul emerges and the individual becomes more loving with each life he lives. It can be said that the ego is necessary for the soul so that it can live in a body here on earth; for example, it is part of an individual's

Viktor

defense system and protects him from dangerous situations.

The task of life is the same in every life—to experience and deal with the emotions that accompany earthly life—and the goal is to develop oneself spiritually and raise one's consciousness steadily. With rising consciousness, the soul gets closer to God's energy. When the soul is in a body along with the ego, it is difficult for the individual to imagine that he is in fact an eternal soul in a mortal body; many people perceive that the body and mind are all that is, and that nothing will take over at the end of life. This is the faith of many, and those who hold this belief fear death, which is, in their consciousness, eternal darkness and silence. It is also difficult to imagine that the soul is a part of everything that is—that it is part of everything that a person sees and feels around him. The earth, nature, and other souls all are one, the unity of all that is.

The individual doesn't really know who he is for a long time, so he often lives in extreme illusions about himself and everything around him. This illusion creates fear and divides people. Sooner or later, everyone will wake up and begin to see through the illusions that are part of earthly life and realize who they are and what the real meaning of life is. First the eyes are opened to the illusions and systems of the world, and then the individual becomes self-conscious and eventually senses who he is and where he is headed. He begins to see life and existence and all people in a different light, and the fear of life and death disappears

Freedom and Shackles

in that person's mind, creating the eternal feeling of freedom.

It is then the task of each person to free their soul from the control of the ego so that their thoughts, actions, and words come from the soul. When the soul begins to control that person's life, it begins to perceive itself as part of everything. The person sees that all the things that divide people here on earth are illusions that lead to unnecessary suffering in humans. Gender, religion, skin color, nationality, and language are temporary things that will all eventually disappear, for eventually souls will be united in the spiritual world to become one entity, and the soul will be united with the energy of God. All the experiences that the soul has gained on the earthly journey become the experience of the whole. Therefore, every moment of every human life is a moment of the whole, and all the experience and wisdom that the soul has acquired is for the benefit of the whole. He who is evil to his neighbor is actually evil to himself and is harming himself, while he who loves his neighbor is actually loving himself.

Therefore, one who perceives that he is part of the unity of everything will begin to change in his attitude toward others. He begins to approach everything and everyone with truth and love. Thus, he will live in God's love and experience it and feel it in his heart. Rude or evil behavior toward others is actually a manifestation of fear. Deception, fear, and division are coherent, since deception leads to fear, which creates divisions among the people. By contrast, love creates unity, tolerance, and compassion among the people, and there is cooperation and helpfulness.

He who has opened his eyes to truth, his heart to love, and his consciousness to unity lives in harmony with the power of God in his body. He has attained spiritual maturity, and his consciousness has reached the highest level. The spiritual world has many levels, of which God's energy is the highest. A person's spiritual development and level of consciousness determine the height to which the soul goes in the spiritual world at the end of that life. He who develops himself spiritually and raises his level of consciousness in life goes upward, thus approaching the God energy from life to life until eventually there is a fusion. Therefore, spiritual development and rising consciousness are the only true success in life. Seeing through self-delusion and living in unconditional love is the highest goal of life for every person, because when it is achieved, he has freed himself from the shackles of deception and fear.

Perceiving oneself as part of everything that is, where everything flows together into one, is the highest and final stage of spiritual awakening and opening. To attain this perception, the ego and the egoistic mind must be sidelined altogether. In achieving this, the individual has perfected his earthly life. This spiritual awakening and opening can take several lives, although there are instances of individuals completing the process in one human lifetime.

Freedom and Shackles

It's all up to each and every one, but one thing is for sure, everyone will end their spiritual opening eventually. It is the spiritual development and state of consciousness that determines when the spiritual awakening begins and ends. No one can force this off or on; everything has its time, and it is wholly about controlling one's mind and thoughts. It is about learning to channel them into love, tolerance, and compassion, learning to love oneself and one's neighbor and all that is, for without this there will be no unity, only continued divisions.

A person who has experienced God's love in his heart begins to thirst for more love and to search for it. This speeds up the journey, because the person becomes addicted to this love and seeks every way to get everyone to live in harmony with the God energy in their bodies. Initially, faith motivates them in their path, but then the experience takes over, and those who have experienced God's love in their heart no longer need to believe.

The world and humans can be challenging to get along with, so it can be difficult at the beginning to feel like part of everything. Many people are fearful, and fear manifests itself in brutal behavior, so it can be difficult to maintain calm and balance among such people. It often tests balance, tolerance, and love for others. With heightened consciousness, you learn to stay calm and balanced in challenging situations and with people who are difficult in their behavior. Such people need love most, because it is fear that drives this behavior. Gradually, you learn to be loving and balanced regardless of your environment and other people. He who is loving carries love and spreads it among others, helping them to ward off fear from their bosoms and creating greater unity among the people of the earth.

There is more in the world today that creates division than constitutes unity among the people. The dominant forces know that a disintegrated group is more easily controllable than a harmonious one, so constantly dividing people through deception and fear is one of their goals. When the masses have opened their eyes to deception and it has ceased to create fear, then the divisions will also cease; the people will begin to stand up and stand together against the ruling powers, and the transformations that lie ahead will go through. Each and every one of us has power and is an important link in a strong chain of unity and love. With solidarity, the era of deception and betrayal will end, and the era of tolerance, cooperation, and love among men will begin. The family will grow stronger, and friendships will be greater among people. Greater calm and balance will come over the world, wars will end, and peace will be established. The state of the world is really a reflection of the consciousness of humanity as a whole, just as an individual's life and environment is a reflection of his or her mind and thoughts. Each person's environment is created by human thoughts.

The transformations that are now sweeping across the earth and mankind are not to be feared. Fear will try to

Freedom and Shackles

hinder and delay many in spiritual opening. But when each person opens his eyes to the truth and his heart to love, thus achieving unity and solidarity among the masses, transformation will become a reality. Each person needs to regain power over himself and his life. Awakening to self-consciousness and learning to control one's mind and thoughts ultimately leads to happiness and a loving life, and this helps to create the great unity among the people here on earth.

Chapter 18

Time of Changing

The changes that are taking place here on earth are, in fact, because humanity is moving out of its youth into adulthood, and thus the attitudes and perceptions of the masses will change. This is an uplift in consciousness and development in the masses. After all, there are souls of all ages here, from the infant stage to the old stage. The young soul's attitudes toward life and existence and other people reflect the attitudes that have prevailed here on earth for centuries. "Life is a competition, and I'm going to beat you no matter what the cost" is the typical attitude of the young soul, and this has been the attitude of the dominant forces and authorities for a long time. During adulthood, the competitive attitude begins to wane, and the individual experiences greater and deeper emotions in his heart. He begins to experience more empathy for others, and helpfulness and tolerance takes over from competition. Communicating with others becomes more important, as does being with others. Adulthood can also be likened to a spiritual awakening, because the individual in this phase begins to perceive himself as part of a larger whole and to take more of an interest in spiritual matters.

In many European countries, there are many adult souls, and life is characterized by their attitudes and outlook. Italy is a good example of such a community where communication with others and connection with family is important. This phase is spiritually challenging in the same way as a spiritual awakening due to inner imbalance and turmoil. It can be said that humanity has distanced itself from its innermost nature of love, unity, and solidarity, which is natural when the attitude is that of the young soul. During this period of man, family values and connections with relatives and close ones are often forgotten. This then changes as the individual matures and becomes an adult and starts a family himself. Then his attitude changes to one of nurturing and cultivating his family and relationships with relatives and friends, and more calm and balance will come into the person's life. This is a simple description of the current era here on earth, in which the attitudes and perspectives of the adult soul are taking over.

These attitudes will also be reflected in the governance structure of the authorities and the dominant forces. The freedom of the people will increase again, and they will be less distressed financially. The old political parties will dissolve, and individuals who care about their fellow citizens will be elected instead, and the aim will now be to help people and make life easier for them as much as

Freedom and Shackles

possible. Until now, this policy has only been in theory and not on the table. More truth and love will prevail among the people as well as between the authorities and the masses. Workloads will decrease, and the family will get stronger again and have more time together.

That energy and execution with a heavy workload are characteristics of the young soul, who has great drive and has drawn others along with him. The United States is a good example of a country where the attitude of the young soul has been dominant. Work comes first, followed by family and then friendship. Fame and fortune are very important to young souls, and they have the drive to get things started and put into practice. This attitude, which has characterized earthly life for centuries, has been challenging for adult and old souls who have had to follow along and have been under heavy workloads for a long time. These older souls prefer a quiet and comfortable life, and they want freedom and free time to enjoy themselves. Similarly, the upcoming season will be a challenging environment for the younger souls, who will find life and existence to be too calm and the attitudes of the masses to be wrong. So it's going to be a challenge for them, but at the same time, it's a path to maturity. Each age of souls can be said to have its favorite period here on earth, but the souls born many times get to experience these periods with different attitudes.

With all change comes tension and imbalance, whether the changes are for good or for evil. This is well perceived here on earth, where there is a great imbalance in nature and climate as well as in the actions of authorities who are trying everything they can to prevent and stop these transformations. Many will act as messengers of truth and love, offering to help people and take charge. Many of these people are wolves in sheep's clothing whose sole intention is to maintain the old system and gain power in their own hands. This will not work, because the eyes of the masses will be opened to the truth that will see through the deceptions, and these individuals will not succeed with their plans.

Many efforts will be made to prevent and stop this transformation, but those who try will not make progress, because it is part of humanity's evolution and process here on earth. Such transformations are rare, occurring every few thousand years, but they are part of the soul's development process. Far out in the future, similar transformations will occur as the average age of souls here on earth moves from adulthood to old, which is the final stage for those souls who came to earth to develop themselves and to experience earthly life.

Despite all the advances of technology and science now and in the future, human nature and structure are always the same. Regardless of environment and technology, the individual must always struggle with himself. His task and goal is to experience, to develop himself spiritually, and to raise the consciousness in slow steps toward God's energy. This goal will remain the same

Freedom and Shackles

as long as man lives here on earth. The stimuli of the environment have varied throughout the different periods the souls have already gone through. Great technological advances in recent decades have led man to become distanced from himself. As a result, thoughts and minds have gone far beyond the individual and often have not resulted in increased spiritual development or rising consciousness but have led to stagnation in the development process of the soul.

It is important that each person be fully self-conscious and learn to control their mind and thoughts, thereby controlling their life and progress. It's easy to be tempted by all the technological advances that have emerged in a short period of time. From the development process of the soul, it can be said that many of the techniques that have emerged are actually stimuli and disruptions of the developmental process. But each person is responsible for himself, and his development and progress depend on each and every one. There is no right or wrong, and there is a time for everything. Many will withdraw from technology and pick up simplicity again, as life was some time ago. This simplicity is about enjoying nature and observing its cycle through the seasons. In this way, man gets closer to himself and his true nature. But man is part of creation and nature, and therefore it is he who provides the balance and inner peace that man is always looking for. Also, people will spend more time together with family, relatives, and friends.

Viktor

Through these transformations, man will find himself again, reconnect with himself, and gain greater self-consciousness. This will happen as soon as the harassment of the authorities and the media subsides, at which point most people will seek balance and gain more calm, peace, balance, and freedom. The pressure will relax people's lives after prolonged harassment and workload, a stress that has hit many. The harassment of the environment and authorities is subtle and insidious, so few realize what it is that causes them great stress, anxiety, worry, and fatigue. For a long time, violence has been mental in nature, and few have seen through the actions of the authorities over the years. But now the truth is coming to the surface, and many will find the reason behind the stress they have been living with for a long time. It will therefore be a great relief when the authorities, the ruling powers, and the high class lose their power over humanity, and the people will gain freedom and peace from all harassment.

Many have given up power to others, to authorities and institutions, and have believed and trusted that the authorities are doing their best to improve people's lives and well-being. The authorities have often abused the power they have been given and greed has taken over, whether it is power grabs or greed for wealth and property. It is important that those who take charge are fearless, are not greedy, do not bully others, and always look out for the good of the whole. But it will be so—the period that is now ending has been part of the development process of the soul, and now other times and new challenges are taking

Freedom and Shackles

place. All that the soul experiences here on earth is part of its development process, whether for good or for evil. This also applies to the different periods and phases through which the soul goes in its long journey here on earth.

Many have already opened their eyes to the truth and are aware of what is happening here on earth. But many are fearful despite seeing the truth in their surroundings; they fear what the authorities will do next to tighten their grip on the people. Then there are others who are unaware of what is happening and have no interest in knowing about it. But most people will go through these changes, whether consciously or unconsciously.

The changes will affect government, monetary systems, taxation, healthcare, education, the media and press, and religion, all of which will be for the better for the people and the masses. Slowly, new systems and new modes will replace the old ones. The freedom of the people will be greatly increased, whether through government reduced regulation or less taxation. The vast majority of people will feel a big difference in their lives and freedoms and embrace this, but there will also be those individuals who are pained to lose their power and wealth. There is a small group of people who have benefited from the system that has been in place for centuries, and this group will have the hardest time with these changes as they fall from the saddle.

The time for family and togetherness has come as materialism and heavy workloads will wane and people will have more free time. This is also the period in which humanity will begin to awaken to self-consciousness and spiritual awakening. Most people will experience greater mental strength and increased intuition. This spiritual awakening leads to internal imbalance, and most people will experience stronger emotions within themselves and thus more emotional vibrations. This will happen as the emotional field becomes more active than before. The number of people who pursue and become interested in spiritual matters will grow, and people will increasingly begin to look inward for truth and love. The creative power of the soul is greatest when it is in adulthood, so creativity of all kinds will be much greater in the times to come. Therefore, spiritual work here on earth will increase, and people will learn their true strength and capacity in the spiritual realm. Much of the spiritual has been hidden from many, as materialism has been dominant and spirituality has been pushed aside. Also, the world system has kept the spiritual down by will. The dominant powers do not want people to gain full spiritual strength and experience a fearless life. Therefore, spirituality has been frowned upon by the system that has prevailed for centuries. But now spirituality will be heard and will become part of people's lives and needs. Cultivating the mind and soul is no less important than cultivating and nurturing the body. When everything is in balance, an individual lives a happy and loving life in his or her body. Everything here on earth and everything that is part of creation ultimately seeks equilibrium, and equilibrium will eventually be achieved.

Chapter 19

Transformations

Regardless of any transformation in an individual's environment, his or her spiritual development and rising consciousness are always up to that individual. A person living in a free environment may feel bonded within, and likewise a person living in external bondage may feel free within. All of this is subjective and a matter of one's attitude toward life. This attitude determines each person in his own mind and thoughts and is therefore a question of individual mindset. Each person needs to find the happiness and joy of life within himself and not let others or anything outside disturb that happiness. Being free from the thoughts, actions, and opinions of others is a great freedom found only within one who is free in his own mind.

Anyone who feels shackled and restrained needs to know that freedom and happiness come from within, and thus spread to others. No one can bring happiness to someone who is unhappy inside. Finding happiness can be helped and guided, but each person finally needs to find it within themselves. He who is free from deception and fear has gained eternal freedom, and nothing outside can take that away from him. Even if the body is in chains, the mind is free.

The transformations that are taking place here on earth are based on spiritual maturity and the rising consciousness of each individual. The frequency of the earth will rise, and thus humanity will follow with a rising consciousness. Each one is an important link in this transformation, and no one is greater than another. Everyone has weight and can contribute if they are ready. In the spiritual worlds, there is no trade-off or division, but merely different soul ages and levels of consciousness. The development of the soul and its level of consciousness occurs in slow and steady steps, almost unconsciously, but every few thousand years the development of the souls mutates, as is happening at present. Such a mutation leads to a huge imbalance in people's lives as major changes take place in the environment and systems of the world. These transformations take a long time in a human lifetime, but only a moment in eternity.

Many people are familiar with the transformations that took place in people's lives and bodies as they transition from young to adult. Great physical changes took place as well as attitudes toward life. These changes can take several years for the person who is a long time out of a lifetime. A lot of internal imbalances and conflicts can arise, whether physical or mental. This passes and most people gain balance in their lives and bodies after that.

Freedom and Shackles

Many are unaware of the conflicts that are taking place on earth, but they sense that something is happening due to the widespread imbalance in world affairs and the upheavals that have arisen. Many people are experiencing more hardship than before, whether financially or in the form of curtailments of freedom, but they do not realize what is causing it. The old systems and their watchmen now struggle day and night to maintain the old system under which the masses have lived for centuries. They do not want to lose their power or bring more freedom and wealth to the masses. The authorities and the ruling powers consider it their power and responsibility to preserve the systems that have served them and the high class for centuries at the expense of the masses. Slowly, the earth and life on earth have changed from freedom to shackles and tribulations, and all this has been done behind the scenes through deception and fraud. People have been led to believe that this is the only thing available to maintain stability and balance in society. The ruling powers absolutely do not want the truth to surface and the people to see and hear how they have managed things for the benefit of the select few. But one thing is certain: the truth will always come to the surface, and it will be difficult for many to face the truth when it finally appears.

There is a large group of individuals who are here on earth to help people wake up and open their eyes to the truth. These are souls who have completed their earthly lives but have come here to assist in this current transformation. These souls are scattered across the earth to carry the message and to help as many people as possible through this period. These souls are hard hit because they receive little recognition in the media and are frowned upon by authorities around the world. There is now a war and a conflict between light and darkness, good and evil here on earth. This same conflict occurs within anyone who is waking up to self-consciousness and spiritual development. But there is a conflict between good and evil at any given time, not least within individuals. Each person must conquer evil and dark within himself in order to gain love in his heart and learn to spread it to others. Good will always triumph in the end, for no power is stronger than love.

The spiritual awakening of the individual is, in fact, humanity's spiritual awakening for the transformations currently taking place here on earth. It's up to each person to participate and contribute. The majority of people need to open their eyes to the truth in order for the transformation to go through. The time this takes is how long the transformation will take. The duration is therefore up to the people: those who have already awakened their consciousness are beginning to wait after the transformation, while the sleeping and blind do not realize what is happening in the world, even though they sense the turmoil and imbalance that is currently prevailing here on earth. Therefore, these are individual transformations, and the chain will never be stronger than its weakest link. Many people sense that time is passing much faster than before; this is due to the rising frequency of the earth, which is

Freedom and Shackles

causing people's attitudes and perceptions to change. The position and course of the celestial bodies and planets influence the frequency and energy here on earth, and the average soul age of humanity can be said to be a reflection of this energy. Many souls want to participate in and experience these transformations, so there are many souls in body here on earth at this time. There are also many souls who leave the earth before the changes take place because they are not ready.

Many people fear any change, whether big or small. Such fear is called stubbornness, and it is one manifestation of fear—the fear of the unknown—so there is conservatism among many who will resist the transformation. But there is nothing to fear, and all will be well after this. Lifestyles, visions, and perceptions change with the aging of souls, just as a person's attitudes and outlook on life change with age. The child and adolescent have a completely different outlook on life than the one who has grown old. Life slows down with age, and it isn't as serious as it was at the beginning. The old man now seeks calm and balance and has learned to enjoy life in the moment. The evolution of humanity and its aging population observe the same laws as the human life. Greater calm and balance will come here on earth at a slow pace. Humans will learn more and become more relaxed, and there will be more calm among the people in the future.

Many will get ahead of themselves and overstep when they gain greater freedom from government regulation, and when the people's finances steadily improve as the authorities decrease taxes and levies. But this will only be for the time being, because everything will then seek equilibrium: people will adapt to this changing environment, and most will appreciate the moderation of freedom and increased wealth. Greater freedom will eventually become natural to the people, who will appreciate it more and more, and it will be difficult to imagine how to live in the old system built on chains, theft, and deception. It can be harder for many to maintain inner calm and balance in success than in adversity, and many people become derailed when they begin to succeed in life and in their careers. The next generation that will be born into a new worldview does not know the old world's sin, so they will experience the new worldview not as greater freedom but as a normal state and environment. Older generations will share the history of the past and what life was like when it was bonded and restrained by a small group of people who held humanity hostage through deception and lies and kept most of them in chains to fear.

Many ideologies have been created by man and presented as a means to a better life for all, where the interests of the whole are the guiding principle and driving force on which the ideology is based. These ideologies relate to politics and to the philosophy and vision that some have of how people should live and be. Yet most of these ideologies basically go out of their way to serve a

Freedom and Shackles

small group of people who draw on the wealth and resources of others, and thus take advantage of their efforts without contributing, and keep people in chains as slaves for a small high class. These times are coming to an end, and there will finally be greater equality, peace, and tranquility here on earth. This will suit the older souls well, as this is their view and outlook on life, but it will not fit well with the younger souls, who view life as competition and have a strong drive and desire to perform and build. In spirituality, everything is equally divided, and all are equal, because there is unity. Class division is a human fabrication: it is in fact in man's nature to live in division and experience oneself as a distinct individual.

It is important to forgive those who have ruled so far. Their mission was to help the souls experience the time that is now coming to an end. Revenge and violence don't solve problems, they make it worse. At the end of his life, each one will face his actions and all that he has done to others, whether good or evil. This is the lesson each person will learn from their lives and actions. The difficult chapter is coming to an end here on earth, and brighter times lie ahead. Those who have reached middle age and above will sense the greatest changes, as they have lived in the old world order all their lives and know nothing else. Accordingly, the changes will have less impact on those who are younger and less familiar with the current old system. Although the changes are positive for most people, they can be difficult for many. It is each person's task to process the changes and find inner balance and happiness in their lives.

Many of those who have had their eyes open to the truth for a long time feel that the authoritarian forces and authorities are allowed to go to great lengths to curtail people's freedom and erode their standard of living, and they have become desperate in their wait for transformation. Many people take a long time to wake up to what is happening in the world. The transformation has already begun and has been going on for many years, but it all happens in slow steps so that nothing is overthrown; the old systems and old values slowly fade away while the new ones come in. This can be compared to a person's spiritual awakening and opening, which can take a long time as old energy in the body is replaced by the love of God's energy. This needs to be done in slow steps so your body doesn't burn out. It takes a long time to change one's mindset and free oneself of the shackles of the mind, fears, and illusions to see through self-deception.

One thing is certain: the transformations that have already begun will go through, and there is nothing earthly or human that can stop it. It is only a matter of time before humanity is ready to take the full step. Many threaten that the earth is about to perish and the end of the world is near, but this is yet another example of creating fear in the masses. Then they make claims about what people need to do to prevent this. These are all illusions that no one needs to take seriously, as one thing is for sure: man will never

Freedom and Shackles

get to destroy the earth, because it affects the solar system and the universe. The energy of celestial bodies and planets, including the earth, is part of a vast whole that needs to be balanced, and man cannot disturb it. When many people talk about the end of the world, what they mean is an end to the old values and systems that have been around for centuries. But there is no end to anything, only transformation. When man dies, the soul leaves the body and continues its journey in another realm, and it will return to earth in another life. What people call death is, in fact, a transition from one to the other and is a natural course of the soul's movement and development.

It is most successful to put your fears aside and observe and experience the transformation. Extreme materialism, which has been the dominant attitude for a long time, will now give way to greater emotion, empathy, and interaction between people. The work week is over, and now the weekend is taking over with free time and spending time with family, relatives, and friends. It will no longer be Monday, but an eternal weekend.

Chapter 20

The True Spiritual Teacher

To assist humanity in its transformation and rising consciousness, there are many souls who have completed their time here on earth and are actually graduates of the school that earth is for the soul. These souls are scattered across the earth, and they help in various ways. Most of these souls lived in deception and fear at first, but at a certain point, they were awakened to the task they came to earth to do. They have to go through a spiritual awakening and opening, just like the souls doing it for the first time. However, they are focused: they move quickly through the spiritual awakening and opening to get ready for the helping work they have undertaken. These souls help humanity in many ways, and their work is very different, although the outcome is the same in all cases. They assist souls with spiritual awakening and opening; they lead the way, educate, and counsel. Many share experiences of their opening and describe the obstacles that can occur on the road and how to overcome them to move forward on one's journey.

All of these helping souls are here to enhance spiritual development and elevate the consciousness of the people.

This is done through books, lectures, and/or private lessons. They also help through their presence, as their energy lifts the energy of those around them. Therefore, many people in this profession are unconscious about their tasks and do good where they come and for those they associate with. Many helping souls work on healing and on sharing information from the spiritual worlds. A true spiritual teacher is one who has personally undergone a spiritual awakening and opening, so he is sharing his own experiences. Accounts from the feelings and experiences of others do not become truth to people until they themselves have experienced them and can express them with conviction, thereby helping others to have the same experience. In this way, help passes on from soul to soul.

There have always been such helping souls here on earth to help mankind along the path to maturity and higher consciousness, to guide and point the way to love, but because of the current transition periods, they are unusually numerous. When a person is ready to wake up to self-consciousness, he will be drawn to the teacher who suits him. That teacher will teach him the way and help him cross its thresholds. But no one can walk another way: each person has to walk his own path and face his own inner challenges and obstacles. The teacher can give advice that eases the journey and makes it more meaningful, but he cannot carry the person over the obstacles along the way. When the individual is ready, he will get all the help and assistance needed. All he must do is plead for help and it will unexpectedly appear in the form of a spiritual teacher

Freedom and Shackles

or a good spiritual book. Each person will feel great enthusiasm and love in his heart once he has found the right mentor. If the teacher creates fear and discomfort in the chest, then he is not the right mentor for that person. It is important to listen to your feelings and intuition when finding a spiritual guide. A true spiritual teacher speaks or expresses himself with his heart and feelings, thereby creating a sense of well-being in the student to which the student is involuntarily attracted. The student begins to thirst for the greater well-being they experience with his teacher, and the teacher will help them to be able to experience this well-being anywhere, at any time, without being in close proximity to the teacher.

The first sign of spiritual awakening is that the person begins to ask himself questions about the meaning of life and who he really is. He begins to sense that not everything is right here on earth and that the systems of the world are inhumane, which they would not have to be if everyone worked together for the well-being of the whole. Many questions and speculations arise, and the person begins to seek answers to all of them. Thus, a spiritual awakening begins step by step, where one thing leads to another. The search for these answers will then draw the person to their spiritual teacher who will assist and lead the way. The person's eyes are opened to the truth about his surroundings and later about himself: "Who am I? What is the meaning of my life and my being here on earth?"

The answers to all these questions will appear to anyone who is willing to wake up to self-consciousness. Later, fear will give way, and love will begin to flow into the body and heart. The person begins to experience the ecstasy of God's energy and senses himself to be home. Eventually, he will perceive that he is part of the unity of all that is. In the end, he will have great compassion and a calling to help others and show them the path he has already been through. Then he himself will become a spiritual teacher who guides others like the guidance he received from his own teacher. Thus, truth and love have been passed from person to person through the centuries and will continue to do so in the same way. This chain will never be broken as long as mankind lives here on earth.

The transformations currently sweeping across the earth and humanity are in fact the transformation of the individual, revolving around his or her spiritual development, attitudes, and rising consciousness; therefore, the transformations are up to each individual. Each person controls when his journey starts and how long it takes. A change in attitude needs to take place so that the individual can experience and participate in the transformation, and the first step is a spiritual awakening and an awakening to self-consciousness. As the frequency of the earth and energy rises, it acts as a catalyst and a calling to the individual, so there are many people today who are opening their eyes to the truth. The position of celestial bodies and planets is also affected, since their position determines the energy field of the earth and

Freedom and Shackles

therefore of humanity. Everything is one and affects each other, whether it be the individual, the earth, or space. Therefore, humanity's spiritual development and consciousness affect the outside world far beyond the earth and the solar system.

He who finds a true and faithful spiritual teacher accelerates his progress, and the spiritual opening becomes more focused. It is important to carefully choose the teacher who is recruited to assist and lead the way. Many teachers start well but later lead the person into dilemmas and dead ends. Each person's intuition is the best measure and compass in this choice. It is also good to see how a spiritual teacher lives and manifests himself in his daily life and to observe whether this is consistent with his teaching. A true teacher is really a role model for others in his life and behavior, and that's really his teaching. A true teacher acts with love and is concerned about the student's movement and well-being. This tutorial can also take the form of books that provide good guidance and help.

Many people are opening up spiritually without even realizing it, so they don't know what is happening. This process is accompanied by physical symptoms as well as mental ones that most doctors are unaware of, so they can provide little assistance. In most cases, such an individual begins to be drawn to spiritual issues and starts searching for educational material in the form of books, films, meetings, and conferences. Finally, the person finds his own path and teacher in his opening, a channel that suits that person. The material the individual chooses to use as guidance on their journey is often determined by how the material is presented. Spiritual teachers and materials are easily accessible online, so people can quickly find out what suits them. Along the way, with increased spiritual development and rising consciousness, the focus and teaching material change. A true spiritual teacher will be able to help and guide that person all the way through the opening as he shares his experience and uses it to teach.

A person who is not ready to awaken to self-consciousness has little or no interest in spiritual matters, and they are hidden from him. He could talk them down and make fun of these matters, but here is the inner fear going around and keeps that person away from looking further into spirituality. An awakening or opening can never be forced if the person is not ready. It happens on each person's own terms when he is ready.

One of the most important things in spiritual awakening and opening is to master the mind and thoughts. Learn to ward off negative and evil thoughts that lead to fear and suffering if they are allowed to grow within you. Learn to have positive and loving thoughts, because this leads to happiness and joy in life. What each person gives away is what they will experience from others in their life. He who is full of evil and hatred will experience the same from others, because people full of similar thoughts will be drawn to that person, and likewise, loving and happy people will adhere to the one who is loving.

Freedom and Shackles

The soul is the divine within each person, and it always guides in the right path in life, leading to great spiritual development and rising consciousness. Whoever has saved the soul within himself will experience the love of God's energy in his heart and thus connect with God and accomplish his mission here on earth. This is the supreme goal of spiritual awakening and opening, and only those who remain steadfast in their search for God will reach that goal. The battle with the ego and false self is challenging, so there are many who postpone the internal conflict and push it off, but ultimately everyone will have the courage and strength to go all the way and free the soul from the control of the ego and false self. A big part of this struggle is a change in attitudes toward life, others, and oneself. He who replaces fear with love in his thoughts gains great freedom and happiness in his life and has freed himself from the shackles of his own mind.

The spiritual awakening and opening of each individual is one of the important foundations of the great transformation of humanity that is now taking place. Every single person is important in that change, and no one is greater or more significant than another. Love will awaken in the heart of men and spread from person to person; truth will conquer illusion, love will conquer fear, and unity will triumph over division, and thus the consciousness of humanity will rise toward the energy of God, the source of all things.

Chapter 21

New Eras

In the past, people had great freedom and cultivated the land, and there were few laws and regulations restricting their freedom. People exchanged goods and services without money or government taxation. Technology in those days was simple, and people were in close contact with nature and collaborated with each other. Although the current transformations on earth are positive for most, these past times will not come again, because everything is transformational, and there will continue to be regulations and money in some form so that people can do business with each other. The current world system has evolved to the point where it now serves the interests of a small group of people ruled by power and greed for money who have been absorbing more and more of the earth's resources and wealth. This has resulted in a steady decline in people's freedom and financial viability. Yet there has also been a great drive and a lot of construction and development among the people, governed by the drive and energy of the young souls.

Each individual is born free in a free world; the resources of the earth are created so that everyone can use them for their own advantage in life, and this innate freedom will be restored to the individual. Also, every person is born with power over himself and his own life and progress, but people have tended to give up that power to others, such as religion or authorities. By electing political parties, an individual gives up his authority to them, believing that they will look after his welfare and life. Many will regain power, become self-conscious, and begin to control their lives and progress. The person giving up power believes and trusts that someone from the outside will give him welfare and happiness. But such happiness is conditional and temporary. Eternal happiness comes from within, radiating out and away from that person. Happiness is independent of everything and everyone, and no one can take it away from someone.

A big part of the transformation is that many will stop trusting the authorities with their lives and progress, because the masses will eventually see through the deceptions that have been used for centuries to privilege the well-being of the high class and a small group of people. Opening one's eyes to the truth is the key to freedom and transformation, and it will happen for many due to the rising frequency and energy of the earth. Many will wonder how great services can be provided to the people through low taxes and levies, because today the smallest part of the taxation by the authorities goes into the service of the people, and the largest part goes to superstructure and administration. This will change, and

Freedom and Shackles

better and more efficient services will be offered in all areas of government.

Many will give up their religion and start looking for other ways to connect with God. Spiritual work will be greatly enhanced as people look inward for happiness and joy in life. More and more people will have a full spiritual opening where their hearts will be opened to the love of God's energy, and fear will thereby depart from their lives. Meditation, healing, and spiritual teaching will take over from religion more and more, and instead of believing, people will experience God's love in their hearts, coming to see and sense that they do not need an intermediary to do so. Thus, the attitudes and perspectives of the masses will change, and the materialism that has existed for a long time will give way to greater emotions and spiritual self-care among the people. Many will feel in their hearts that spiritual maturity and rising consciousness are the only true value of life, the eternal treasure that will follow the soul from life to life to the end, when it will be reunited with the energy of God after a long journey and many lives here on earth. The holiday season will be valuable to people, so materialism will gradually give way to other values. The greedy and ruling powers will struggle with these changes, as this goes against their vision and beliefs, and therefore the transformation will be very difficult and challenging or this group of people as well as for others.

All changes, whether positive or negative, are tense and create imbalances while they pass. This period is therefore challenging for the masses, but once transformation is over, equilibrium will be restored, the new world will begin to take shape, and human systems will adapt to the changes in people's attitudes to live.

Many people are exhausted from the stress that exists here on earth. The workload is great and there are high demands on people, not least the children. The flow of information has become vast and constant, and many people have become dependent on phones and computers to monitor everything that goes on. Much of this information provides little spiritual development or higher consciousness, but only distracts people's attention from themselves, and people thus give up power to these devices. Man has therefore distanced himself from his true self with great speed in recent years, so many are off track in their lives and missing out on the maturity they intended to attain in life. It is natural to cultivate oneself, to gain self-consciousness and mastery of one's mind and thoughts, and to be in touch with nature, and thus each person will attain great spiritual development and eternal success. Therefore, it is good for each person to stop and look at themselves and their life from a distance and see if this is the path they want to take in their life. "Is this the life I want to live, and is this life giving me happiness?" It is up to each person to wake up to self-consciousness and learn to create the happiness and joy they deserve. Everyone is God's child and deserves only the best in their lives. Each one is the captain of his own yacht, although many are unaware of this and give up their power to others.

Freedom and Shackles

The time for spiritual maturity and rising consciousness has come, and this coming period can be said to be a spiritual awakening and opening for mankind. The adult stage of the life of the soul is a period of spiritual awakening and opening, at which point the person begins to look inward and pursue spiritual development rather than the drive for fame that characterizes the young stage of the soul. Spiritual awakening and opening are accompanied by internal imbalances and disorders due to the changes that are taking place. Today's medical science knows little about what is happening, so many people get treated incorrectly. Often it is classified as a mental illness of some kind, and in many cases, it is resolved with medication that inhibits and slows mental opening.

What can be called spirituality is hidden from science; this has been done with a willingness to keep people from the truth and their true selves, because the authorities would lose control of such a person and no longer be able to govern through deception and fear. It is no coincidence that spirituality is not part of today's education or health care system. One of the things that will change in the coming times is that the spiritual aspect of man will become part of his health, and physicians will gain knowledge about this part of man. Today, spiritual teachers, mentors, and healers are best placed to help people through spiritual awakening and opening. The accompanying ailments and side effects are temporary; the person will eventually regain internal balance and calm, and in fact much greater he has experienced before.

Spirituality and meditation will become part of children's education and medical science, thus helping everyone to gain their full strength, mental as well as physical. Instead of serving the interests of a small group, the system will begin to work for the economy of the whole and will be governed by all people here on earth. The fact that someone is suffering from a shortage in today's world is the decision-making of a few individuals. Many will find it hard to believe what the authorities and the system can do when the decision is made to work for the good of the masses. Then all aspects of society will begin to be built up for the benefit of all instead of the artificial restrictions that exist now.

There are big changes ahead for humanity, and they will take time, because if they happen too quickly, there will be a collision. This process of change is governed by the same laws as the spiritual awakening and opening of an individual, which occurs over a long period of time to prevent the body and mind from burning out. Similarly, the old systems under which humanity lives today will fade away, and new ones will come in slowly. The result is that humanity will gain more freedom than it has experienced for centuries. The need for money will diminish, and therefore workloads will be reduced. People will gain wisdom and spiritual maturity in the education system. Healthcare will improve and increase significantly, and it will be quite different from what it is now. Rulers will look to the good of the masses instead of a select few. More equilibrium will be achieved, and trade-offs will be

Freedom and Shackles

reduced. A greater balance between weather and nature will be achieved. The individual will begin to cultivate himself more, physically as well as mentally, and the spiritual development and consciousness of many will increase significantly. There will be more love and compassion among people through greater cooperation. All the harassment that is plaguing many people today will diminish; more calm will come over the world and humanity, and world peace will be brought about after centuries of human war.

Chapter 22

The Unity of All That Is

The life span of man, the age of the soul, and the period of humanity are all structured in the same way and subject to the same laws. Man is born and becomes an infant, later a child, a young person, an adult, and then an old person, and eventually the soul leaves the body at the end of his life and that life is thus over. Man has different attitudes and outlooks on life in each stage: the young man has completely different visions and desires than the old man who has reached the end of his life. The infant needs a lot of care, the young child needs teaching and discipline, and the adolescent is on the verge of becoming an adult, so they have a lot of internal uneasiness over the years. Adults are raising children and setting up a home; the person is slowing down, and she has established a home and started enjoying life with family, relatives, and friends. She now has more time to cultivate herself and her family ties. Then, when the person gets old, life slows down dramatically, and the person seeks calm and balance. The old person has learned to enjoy life, as well as gardening and quiet. This is essentially a person's life as seen from different ages, although nothing is absolute.

The soul comes from the energy of God as one particle from it, and the output of the soul is therefore the same as the consciousness of God's energy: truth, love, and the unity of all that is. The soul goes to earth to experience all that earthly life has to offer, and on its journey from life to life, it gets to experience its opposites, which are deception, fear, and division. There are so many things to experience on earth and so much to learn, so the soul comes to earth hundreds of times before finally returning to the God energy where it came from. The experience of each soul is the experience of the whole; therefore, all are equally important, none more so than another.

In order to gain the most varied experience, the soul goes through an age cycle and has different attitudes and visions of life at every epoch, just like man in his lifetime. Each soul lives many lives in each stage to experience all that each age course has to offer. She starts out as an infant soul, helpless, and takes her first steps into a body. Then she goes through a childhood phase where she needs discipline and regulation to thrive, like the child disciplined in her upbringing. Then comes the youth phase with great energy and execution: at this point, life is competition, and worldly wealth and fame are important. Greed often dominates in order to acquire the best and win the quality-of-life race. Then, in adulthood, family relationships and communication take over from the young soul's quality-of-

Freedom and Shackles

life race, cooperation takes over from competition, and the individual begins to examine himself; as he opens spiritually, spiritual issues become part of life.

Eventually the soul grows old and lives a slow life, avoiding much hustle and bustle; she feels comfortable gardening and has learned to relax and enjoy life. She is not afraid to die, because she now knows that she is a part of everything. The quality-of-life race is over, and communication with others is balanced. The individual has become spiritually strong and has begun to control his mind and thoughts, thereby controlling his life and progress for the benefit of the soul and the whole. In the last lives of the soul, the individual has entered self-karma and tends to withdraw as much as possible from other people, often choosing to live alone and remotely, allowing time and privacy for introspection and self-cultivation. Finally, the soul completes its earthly life and becomes spiritual for a long time until it eventually merges with the God energy from which it originated. He who has understood and accepted that he is an eternal soul in a mortal body has attained great spiritual maturity and high consciousness.

The average age of souls here on earth follows the same epochs as the life cycle of man and the age of each soul. At present, the average age of souls and therefore of humanity is moving from youth to adulthood. This connection between human life, the age of souls, and the period of humanity shows how all are interconnected and obey the same laws. Everything inside each person will be reflected in their life and surroundings, as each person creates their own life and setting with their thoughts. The battle between good and evil, light and darkness takes place within each person as well as in life itself, and the battle between good and evil takes place all over the world.

It is intended that man perceive himself as a distinct individual among other individuals, and it is the role of the ego to create this experience and outlook on life. Communication and emotions are a big part of the soul experience here on earth. As the soul ages and is well into adulthood and later the old phase, the influence of the ego diminishes, and the soul takes more and more control of the person's life. With the soul comes truth and love, and the individual perceives himself as part of all that is. He senses that the soul is part of all souls and everything around him. Thus, the individual becomes more loving and tolerant as the soul ages. Fear and all its manifestations disappear, and an individual learns not to fear life or death.

When your eyes are opened to the truth from the outside, and it becomes apparent how a small number of people have long stolen the freedom, time, and resources of the masses, it is important not to become filled with hatred and anger. He who rewards evil with evil only makes evil worse. Those in this small group are also children of God on their journey of the soul, and they will eventually also be united with God's energy in truth and love. It is best to pray for these people that they may find their way

Freedom and Shackles

to love. Their actions are manifestations of fear—fear of losing their power and wealth. Therefore, it is these people who need a lot of help to escape the shackles of self-deception and fear. From God's perspective, there is no evil and no good; everything is, and is part of the development process of the soul. In order for humanity to experience the different periods here on earth, individuals are needed to create the often-challenging conditions. As was said, whoever judges will be judged, and that is fitting in this case, because everyone has their part in the play of life.

He who has understood and accepted that all is one has gained a deep understanding of himself, of other people, and of life and existence. His eyes are open to the truth, and his heart is open to the love of God's energy. He understands and perceives each person, seeing where they are in their career and on their journey. He perceives all the obstacles he is going through, and he sees the bigger picture. He has gained a lot of tolerance and is willing to help those in trouble. He who understands and perceives the unity of all things has attained the highest level of spiritual opening: he has connected to the God energy in his heart and body, and thus he has completed his earthly life. This can only be achieved by loving oneself and others unconditionally, as by this time, the mind is pure and free from all fear and illusion. This is the eternal freedom that no one can take or steal from anyone, a freedom that has come to be independent of external circumstances.

Although many at this time will open their eyes to the truth on the outside and see through the deception of the authorities and the media, few will go further and come to understand and accept the unity of all things. But even if it doesn't happen in this life, it will happen later, because everyone will understand and sense the unity eventually—it is everyone's mission to go through a spiritual awakening and opening. It is part of the movement of the soul and its natural development and improvement. But for the transformation to take place and the old systems to be removed from the new, the masses need to see the illusions in order to reject the old systems. It is therefore necessary for the masses to open their eyes to the truth.

The eyes of many people will open without any warning or effort, and this will happen unconsciously: suddenly the illusions will become obvious, and there is no avoiding seeing them. Once the eyes are opened, they do not close again, and the truth becomes clearer and more obvious each day. The natural response is to be filled with anger, hatred, and fear of what will happen next. After a certain period of time, love begins to come to that person; they gradually gain the deep understanding that lifts them out of negative feelings and thoughts, and they begin to build up and strengthen themselves. Then those who have gone through this process are invited and equipped to assist people through this period of opening.

This journey and this process of man has been part of the soul's journey from the beginning and will remain this

Freedom and Shackles

way until the very end. Regardless of all technological advances and changes in the world, the structure of man has always remained the same. The only thing that changes is the rising consciousness each soul acquires through its aging process and the spiritual maturity it acquires on its way from life to life. All the time the soul is in a body here on earth, it is always searching for its origin and home. People use different approaches at first in their search, many of which yield little results. Most people look for happiness and love in their hearts and lives. One thing is for certain: all souls will eventually find and merge with God's energy, and this will happen after many lives with different challenges and obstacles that they have overcome in order to develop and improve. The number of lives and the time it takes the soul to find its home again is up to each one and can vary widely. Some souls move quickly and develop full maturity and awareness in a few lives, while others live more lives and move more slowly. As was said, he who is last will be first, and he who is first will be last, which applies to this description. Only those who have opened their eyes to truth and their heart to love, and who have understood and received the unity of all things, have attained the conscious level of God's energy. They are not deceived; they are free from fear in all its manifestations, and they are free from all deception. They live in harmony and rhythm with the energy of God and thereby unite with it in their bodies. There are few people at any given time who find this, but it will be found eventually by anybody who has a burning desire and starts searching.

Printed in Great Britain
by Amazon